FOR
WINSTON AND JUDY

HOW TO WIN YOUR AUDIENCE WITH HUMOR

Winston K. Pendleton

Pireaus Publishers
St. Louis, Missouri

ISBN: 0-913656-02-X
copyright © 1969 by Winston K. Pendleton
Published as a special edition by Pireaus, a division of Forum
Press, Box 179, St. Louis, Mo. 63166.
Library of Congress Catalog Card Number 77-077057

Printed in the United States of America

Cover and illustrations by Robert Naujoks

CONTENTS

GREETINGS!

This book tells you HOW, WHY, and WHEN to put humor in your speeches.

Humor in public speaking works like salt, spices and herbs in cooking. The proper seasoning can change a tasteless dish into a gourmet's delight. Humor can turn a dull speech into a standing ovation.

As in cooking, where the degree of perfection depends on the proper ingredients and the skill of the chef, successful humor depends on how well your stories fit your speech and your ability to tell them.

In the following pages you will find how humor can make a speech sparkle and win an audience. You will learn how to tell a funny story for its greatest impact. You will discover ways to improve your storytelling techniques. Included are many examples of humorous stories, anecdotes and quips that you can use.

This book is not designed to turn you into a nightclub comedian, but it will help you create merriment and laughter the next time you are called on to speak.

WINSTON K. PENDLETON

I
WHAT HUMOR CAN DO

Humor is the single most powerful card in the hand of a public speaker—it can make the difference between a winning speech and a lost evening. Humor can win many a trick for you if you take the time to learn how to play it properly.

Here are the principal ways in which humor can be used in a speech from the moment you are introduced until the time you step down from the dais.

YOUR OPENING

Professional public speakers with long years of experience will admit that the most crucial minute of a speech

1

is the minute immediately following the introduction.

There are five distinct functions that humor can perform during those important opening moments.

To attract attention. Nothing will capture the attention of an audience as quickly as a genuinely funny story. There are times when you will find an ideal situation— the audience quietly expectant, with all eyes turned in your direction as you step up to the lectern. Unfortunately, this is not always the case. More often you will face an audience where people are still engaged in conversation with their neighbors or are moving their chairs about to get more comfortable. They may be in the midst of eating their desserts or lighting cigarettes. You might even be introduced while some of the waitresses are still clearing the tables.

Your job is to get the audience's attention immediately. A funny story can help you do it. If ten percent of your listeners are not paying attention, and suddenly the other ninety percent burst into peals of laughter, you'll have the attention of the entire group by the time the laughter has died down.

To create expectancy. Once a wave of laughter has swept the hall and you have seized the audience's attention, you will discover that your humorous opening story has performed a second function. Not only has it attracted attention, it has also created an air of anticipation throughout the room. Everyone is waiting for you to raise another laugh. They are eager to hear what you are going to say next. This is the ideal moment to reward them with another funny story. If your second joke goes over, you will have the audience exactly where you want it—waiting expectantly for your next words.

To build rapport. Suddenly you will discover that something else has happened to your audience. They are warmer and more friendly toward you. You have achieved

2

the most difficult of all tasks for a speaker. Within a few minutes you have established a perfect rapport with the folks out front. Now that you have a roomful of friends, a quip or another touch of informal humor can accomplish an additional task—helping the audience to relax.

To relax your audience. When a friend drops by your home for a chat, you want to make him feel relaxed and comfortable. In the wintertime you might seat him in your most comfortable chair before the fire; in the summer months you might suggest that he take off his coat and tie and have a cool refreshment. All of these acts are designed to make him feel at ease and contented. Humor is the best means for helping an audience to relax.

To condition yourself. While you have been attracting attention and getting your audience into the proper frame of mind to listen to your speech, something has also been happening to you, although you may not be aware of it. In the process of making your listeners feel comfortable, you have been giving yourself the same sort of treatment. Nothing is more stimulating for a speaker than to hear an audience roar with laughter. When this occurs you will discover that you too are relaxed—your tensions and nervousness have disappeared.

Now you are ready to move into the main part of your speech with you and your audience perfectly attuned to one another.

THE BODY OF YOUR SPEECH

Once you feel that you have your audience in a receptive mood and that you yourself are ready, swing into your speech but always keep humor in mind. There are several other ways in which humor can help you throughout your entire speech.

To help hold attention. Holding the attention of an

audience is equally as important as capturing it in the first place. A well-placed funny story here and there will capitalize on the air of expectancy that you have created. It will help you sustain the interest of your listeners throughout your speech.

To help dramatize a point. If your funny stories have been carefully chosen, they will do more than merely hold attention. They will illustrate and clarify the main points of your address. A good format to follow is to tell a funny story at the beginning or the "top" of the point you are going to make. In that way your message will have a greater impact and a more lasting effect.

For example, suppose you are starting the portion of your speech that deals with quality merchandise. You want to make the point that while anyone can cut corners and sell a product for less, quality is a more important consideration than price. You begin with this story: "A woman in our neighborhood went to see a plastic surgeon about changing the shape of her nose. 'How much will it cost for you to change the shape of my nose?' she asked. The doctor told her three hundred dollars. 'Three hundred dollars!' she said. 'That's a lot of money. Isn't there something less expensive?' 'Well,' the plastic surgeon said, 'you might try running into a telephone pole.'" Later, when you have made your point and have said all you have to say on the subject of quality merchandise, you can come back to your funny story and reemphasize the point by saying, "So remember: If you want something cheaper, there's always a way to get it. Like the plastic surgeon told the lady, 'You might try running into a telephone pole.'"

To keep your audience alert. Using humor to dramatize your message has the added virtue of keeping an audience on the edge of their seats and alert. And nobody can fall asleep in that position. A person who might not be particularly interested in listening to what you have to say about quality merchandise (he thinks he knows all about it) will, nevertheless, pay attention because he wants to hear how you are going to tie in the story about the lady running into the telephone pole.

To help the audience follow you. When you illustrate your points with humor, you will not only keep your listeners awake, but you will enable them to follow you from topic to topic more easily and willingly.

It is not always easy for an audience to follow a speaker's train of thought. The speaker may move from subject to subject faster than his audience can adjust, or his transitions may be weak. Perhaps the speaker has made his point so interesting that the listener refuses to get his mind off it and follow on to the next point. The latter, by the way, is not an unusual situation. The speaker may deliver his remarks so effectively that he sets up a powerful train of thought in the mind of a listener. That man may sit and pursue the idea for some minutes, not hearing another word that the speaker is saying. Nothing is as useful as a bit of humor to shatter the preoccupation of one of these nonlisteners and make him attentive to the rest of your speech.

YOUR CLOSING

Most speakers find it difficult to bring their talk to an end. More often than not they hem and haw, murmur several "thank yous" or "good-byes," and generally behave in an awkward manner.

Here again humor can come to the rescue. It can play two important roles in helping you to bring your speech to a fitting close.

To help you end dramatically. No set of words is as final or as conclusive as the punch line to a funny story.

Once the punch line has been delivered, there is nothing more to say. There is nothing more that needs to be said. The dramatic words are out and the laughter will come roaring in. On the other hand, it is not always easy to choose the right closing words for a speech. Moreover, closing remarks in general don't usually generate an immediate and spontaneous reaction. The speaker then feels that he must add one more sentence, and then another, until at last his speech has no clear-cut conclusion —it just peters out. Humor will solve that problem. If you slide gracefully into an appropriate funny story for a closing, you will find that the audience will applaud and laugh at the same time, and that you will receive a much greater final ovation than otherwise.

To make an audience remember you. If you are skillful enough to have everyone in the audience leave the room with a smile on his face and a laugh in his heart, you will be remembered. Sometimes the people who heard your speech will even remember what you had to say. And what more can a speaker ask for?

THE COVER-UP

There is one other way in which humor can come to the aid of a speaker. Humor allows a skilled speaker to "cover up."

An accomplished storyteller can give people the impression that he has delivered a great speech when in truth he didn't have much to say or when he came poorly prepared and made a bad speech.

When this happens, humor helps the speaker make a successful "nonspeech." Shame on you if you do it.

II
HOW TO TELL
A FUNNY
STORY

Have you ever wondered why one speaker can regale an audience with a funny story and another person, telling the same story, will lay an egg?

The answer is simple: how. How the story was told.

How a story is told is more important than the story itself or the mood of the audience.

There is a variety of ways to deliver funny stories—some people prefer to stand up, others to sit down; some speakers perform in elaborate costume; others wear street clothes. Some people shout the funny lines; others whisper them.

Regardless of the storytelling technique, if the audience responds with laughter, you can be certain that two basic principles have been followed.

The two keystones for telling a funny story properly are: First, you must know your story. Second, you must make it sound like the truth.

Of course, there are several other elements involved in the delivery of stories, but if you don't understand the basics, you'll never be able to master the succeeding steps.

This chapter explains how to select the proper story for your particular needs. It discusses how to learn the story so that you will be able to tell it without ever making a mistake. You will learn how to be convincing before an audience—that is, what you must do to make a story sound like the truth. You will discover some of the secrets of professionals for managing an audience. These pointers will help you "milk" the laughter from the crowd once you have them "with you" and laughing. Finally, there is a detailed plan for the most important step in developing your skill as a storyteller—practice.

Being able to tell a funny story is not a gift. It is a technique, a "how to" that can be learned and perfected.

Study this chapter over and over again. Practice the techniques as they are outlined. Do this and you too will learn how to tell a funny story and make people laugh.

WHAT STORY TO TELL?

The first step in your preparation is learning to select the right story for the right occasion. Whether the story, anecdote or quip is to be used as an opener or a closer or to illustrate a point in your speech, you are always looking for a story that will tickle the audience's funny bone.

Be sure the story is funny. If you don't think it is funny, don't use it. Perhaps you heard another speaker tell the story at a meeting with hilarious results. And you said to yourself, "I didn't think it was all that funny, but if he got a laugh with it, so can I." Don't make that mistake.

This is going to be your story. You are going to tell it. You must understand what is funny about it and you must think it is funny. If you attempt to make people laugh at a story that you yourself don't consider funny, then you certainly won't be able to convince them. It is hard enough to succeed with a story you really enjoy, so don't attempt the impossible.

There are many sources of humorous stories. One of them is stories told by other speakers. In such cases, you not only find a new story, you also get an impression of how (or how not) to deliver it. One word of caution, though. Be careful not to tell the story in the same general working area of the man from whom you "borrowed" the story.

Probably the best sources of stories are humor reference books, which can be found in any public library. The best books are organized like dictionaries, with the stories listed by subject and cross-referenced.

When you are looking for a story to fit your speech, you should always consider what people laugh at—and what they don't laugh at. People like to laugh at other people. People who are suffering or in genuine misery are to be pitied and their situations are not humorous. On the other hand, people do laugh at individuals who get into predicaments or embarrassing situations due to their own stupidity or gullibility or conceit or overeagerness, or some other similar failing.

People like to see smart alecks and conceited and pompous individuals get their comeuppance. They roar when they see the "I'm always right" type of person proved wrong. Jack Benny, for example, is a marvelous storyteller. When you laugh at him you are laughing at the always-trying-to-be-clever person who always loses out.

In looking for a funny story, try to find one that puts the principal character in a ridiculous situation. Obviously, the best person to play the role of the embarrassed dunce is you. Next in order come people in the community who are well known and well liked. If you are speaking at a banquet, you will always get a big laugh with a story told about the man who introduced you or the president of the group. You are also on safe ground when you poke good-natured fun at the audience or at the association that has invited you to speak. For example, if you are addressing a convention of television repairmen you might say, "I really don't know why I was invited to speak to you people. I don't know any more about repairing a television set than you do."

If your aim is to provoke laughter, remember that the humor in the story must be evident and easy to grasp. Subtle humor may be quite witty, but few audiences laugh at it. If your listeners have to figure out what they are supposed to laugh at, they won't laugh.

Many speakers make the mistake of trying to get the audience to laugh at cleverness. A good example of clever humor is the pun. When a public speaker concentrates his humor on puns, he is saying in essence, "Look how clever and smart I am. I thought up a bright saying." Audiences don't laugh at puns. Smart quips rarely raise much laughter for two reasons: first, they sound as if the speaker is trying to be smart; and second, a quip generally comes so quickly that the audience doesn't have time to grasp its humor.

In selecting a story, then, be sure that you think it is funny and that the humor can be easily appreciated. If all of this sounds a bit complicated, there is one element in humor that is always in your favor. Humor is ageless. As long as a story fits smoothly into your speech, the age of the joke is unimportant. Many speakers today are getting belly laughs with stories that were told by Abraham

Lincoln and Grover Cleveland. And you can be sure that they didn't think up all of their own stories either.

LEARN YOUR STORY

Once you have found a story you like, you must learn it so well that it becomes a part of you. To become a part of you, it must sound like you. This means that you have to rewrite the story in your own words until it becomes *your* story and not somebody else's warmed-over joke.

You will find that reworking a story is also the best way to learn it.

You must rewrite the story for it to sound like the truth when you tell it. You must deliver it in your own words, common words that you use in everyday conversation. Never use phrases or expressions that have been obviously taken from a book.

Rewrite the story as if it happened to you or you were present when the event occurred. To make the story ring true, it must seem to be a part of your own experience. You are going to tell the story from firsthand experience, not as hearsay.

Here is an example of what we are talking about. Properly told, this story will appeal to any adult audience. First, it is quoted exactly as it was written in a well-known joke dictionary. Next, we have rewritten the story the way you might have if you had selected it for your speech.

As it was printed in the book:

A fellow had finished his breakfast and had put on his hat and coat and was leaving the house to go to work when his wife kissed him good-bye and said, "Honey, don't you remember what day this is?" He didn't remember, but he didn't say anything. He just hurried off to work. But he thought about it all day long and that night on the way home he stopped in the store and spent about twenty dollars on a gift. As he walked in the front door he said, "Honey, look what I bought you in honor of this great day." "My goodness," his wife said, "this is wonderful. This is the happiest Ground-hog Day I can ever remember."

As you have rewritten it for telling—and why.

One of my biggest problems is not being able to re-member things—mainly anniversaries. [There are three items to note here. First, you have established rapport with most of the men in your audience. All of them forget things now and then and most of them have for-gotten an anniversary at one time or another. They sympathize with you and appreciate your problem. Second, you are explaining what the story is going to be about—forgetting anniversaries. Third, note the use of the word "mainly." "Particularly" would be a good word, but it is too hard to pronounce. Use "mainly" or "especially" or some other word that is part of your everyday vocabulary. The story must sound like you; it must ring true.] Not long ago, I was putting on my coat to leave the house for work [This makes it sound like the truth without your having to stop and say, "This is a true story." You are preparing to relate a personal experience] when Mary put her arms around my neck and kissed me good-bye and looked up at me with a pitiful look on her face and said, "Don't you remember what day this is?" I didn't remember what day it was. [But you immediately thought that you had forgotten another anniversary, and the audience is reading your mind. They are right with you. That is the reason you started the story by saying you had a habit of forgetting anniversaries.] And I did what every smart man in this room would do. I pretended I didn't hear her, and got out of the house. But, boy, did I worry! So about ten-thirty I called the drugstore and asked them to send a two-pound box of candy to my house. [You are creating a little more suspense than the man who wrote the original story.] I still couldn't remember what day it was, so about noon I sent four dozen roses home. [A little more suspense.] But I never did remember what day it was, so on the way home I went into a shopping center and bought my wife something pretty and had it gift-wrapped. And when I went in the front door, I said, "Look, honey. Look what I bought you." And she rushed up to me and threw her arms around my neck and kissed me and said, "Oh, this is wonderful. This is the happiest Groundhog Day I can ever remember." [You will notice that the man who wrote the joke dictionary had a perfect punch line. This is the only line of the story that you should use exactly as it was written. You might be able to improve on it, but I think it would be difficult.]

In rewriting this story, you have retained a laugh-getting punch line and have built a more elaborate story around it. There is, however, one danger in this technique. Be careful not to talk too much. Don't add a lot of irrelevant information. Adding the right amount of information will build up suspense; but extraneous material will make the story drag and destroy its impact.

For example, adding that you sent home a box of candy and then flowers and finally bought a special gift makes the audience believe that the day must have been a very important one. However, don't add words merely to draw out the story in time; that is, details about the weather or what your wife was wearing or the fact that the candy was delivered in person by the pharmacist.

A good rule to follow is to keep on the subject and make every sentence relate directly to the punch line. Make everything you say relevant to the point of the story.

In selecting material, don't overlook short, one-sentence jokes. Sometimes they too can be rewritten and expanded into minor masterpieces. Here is an example of a short story that might not sound too promising at first glance. However, it can be developed into a production that will bring down the house at any formal dinner where you are speaking and your wife is sitting alongside you at the head table.

As the story was found in a book:

A man said to his friend: "My wife and I have enjoyed seventeen years of perfect married happiness. I think that's pretty good considering we have been married thirty years."

As you have rewritten the story—and how you tell it. (You might use it after the one about Groundhog Day):

The reason I told that story was to bring a certain person a big surprise this evening. I forget so many anniversaries that I am very proud when I do remember one. I have remembered this one. If you folks will excuse me for being a bit personal, I would like my wife. Mary, to stand up. I want to say that tonight she and I are celebrating seventeen years of perfect married happiness. [Act as though it were the truth. You must look at Mary with adoration in your eyes. If she is seated next to you, you might even help her to her feet. She must stand up and smile at the audience. If you do it well, their natural reaction will be to applaud.

14

They never fail. After their applause has died down and your wife is seated, you again speak to them.] Thank you so much. I thought it was pretty good my-self—seventeen out of thirty.

You will notice that in this case you have improved on the original punch line. With your revised punch line, your expanded version of the story has everything that a winning story should have. To begin with, it is personal. You have invited the audience to share a joyous experi-ence with you. They, in turn, have feelings of warmth and friendship for you. Then with a single sentence you do two things. You surprise them. And you pull the rug out from under them. The audience suddenly discovers that this is a joke. The joke is on them. This knowledge comes as a complete surprise.

Surprise is one of the most important elements in pro-voking laughter. Suppose, for example, that you had an act where a waiter comes out of the kitchen with a huge cake and stumbles with it. It could be hilarious. If you announced ahead of time that the waiter was coming out of the kitchen with a cake and that he was going to fall down with it, you would ruin the entire routine by re-moving the element of surprise.

When you write and rework your stories, be sure they suit your personality. Be sure they contain the magic ele-ment of surprise. Be careful to tell them in language that you use. Keep them short and to the point.

Which brings us to a word about telling stories in dia-lect. Unless the dialect is part of your own background, don't use it. A dialect in itself is not funny. It is only win-dow trimming to make a story seem more authentic. If you are from the South and have a southern accent, you might very well tell a story using the dialect. This is ac-ceptable if it helps to make the story ring true.

On the other hand, if a native Bostonian tried to deliver a story with a Southern accent, the story would lose any semblance of truth—and much of its punch would be gone. Or can you imagine a fellow from Tennessee or Mississippi trying to imitate a member of the British House of Lords—and getting away with it?

If you are a city lawyer who was reared on a farm and you are relating an event that happened to you when you were a boy, it is perfectly all right for you to swing into your boyhood vernacular.

By the time you have rewritten the story in your own style and have tailored it to the speaking occasion, you will know it. It will have become your story. You will have learned it well enough to tell it before any audience.

Then, when you have mastered the techniques that are discussed further on in the book, you will have a surefire laugh-getter every time you tell it.

BE CONVINCING

Sincerity is one of the most important factors in your success as a public speaker. The sincere man who stammers will make a more persuasive presentation than an eloquent hypocrite.

Your humor must be as sincere as every other part of your speech, if it is to be convincing. Humor must have the ring of truth.

If you want your funny story to come alive, relate it as though it were an event, trial or tribulation that you had actually experienced. In order to make it sound like the truth, you yourself must believe it. Consider your funny story as fact. Think of it as an actual happening. You must sound as though you are eager to tell your friends about an exciting personal experience. If you do not believe in your funny story, you will never be able to convince your audience to believe it.

There are several storytelling techniques that will help to make you sound convincing. Practice them and your humor will seem sincere and truthful.

Your speech is in the first person; therefore, your humor should be presented in the first person too.

Instead of saying, "There is a story about two teen-age boys who were talking to each other . . ." inject your personality into the story and present it this way: "The other evening I overheard my teen-age son talking to a friend of his who had come by the house. My son was chiding him about being girl crazy. 'All you do is chase girls,' my son said to him. 'Don't you know what the poet said about girls? He said a girl is nothing but a rag, a bone and a hank of hair.' And my son's friend stuck out his hand and said, 'In that case, shake hands with the biggest junk collector in school.'"

First-person humor brings you close to your listeners. They are looking at the person who experienced the situation. Third-person humor creates a barrier between you and the audience. They have to imagine the principal character in the story.

When you want to win your audience, tell a "true" story on yourself. Depict yourself in an embarrassing situation. For example, "The other night after I had finished making a speech I overheard a lady say to her husband, 'That certainly was an inspirational speech, wasn't it?' And her husband said, 'It was all right, but thirty minutes of rain would have done us a lot more good.'" Everybody enjoys laughing at the speaker, so tell a lot of stories on yourself. It is always easier to make them sound convincing.

If you tell a story that you enjoy and deliver it in the first person, you will find that it is easy to involve yourself in it. Enthusiasm and eagerness will make a story sound important and convincing. Tell the story as though you were there, as though you saw it happen, or as though you were in the middle of it.

Make the story sound exciting. If you are excited about it, you will transmit your enthusiasm to the audience. If you deliver a story without color or zest, you'll only bore your listeners and no one will laugh.

Speak loud enough to be heard by everyone and speak distinctly. Be sure everyone understands what you are saying. Many a story has been ruined because the lines were not given clearly, distinctly and deliberately.

Be dramatic. Wave your arms and act out any part of the story that lends itself to dramatization. For example, "The other night I dreamed I went fishing. That was some dream. I dreamed that two striptease dancers went along with me. One to row the boat and the other to put the bait on my hook. That was some fishing trip. I caught an eight-pound bass." (Say it as though this was the greatest accomplishment of your life. Hold up your hands to measure the size of the fish.)

Acted out, the story will sound convincing. Your listeners will believe that you really did have such a dream—and that you are also a bit dull-witted. Put the two together and the result will be a belly laugh.

MANAGING THE AUDIENCE

Laughter is contagious. It is infectious. With one or two hysterical members in an audience, you can soon have the entire roomful of people laughing.

Have you ever noticed how one giggling youngster, apparently laughing at nothing in particular, can set off waves of uncontrolled laughter? It appears to be some sort of released emotional explosion, which generally happens at school or in church. Adults are subject to the same phenomenon.

This seems to be especially true of women. Women may not have a better sense of humor than men, but certainly they are less inhibited with their laughter. An auditorium filled with men can make for a great audience. Add a few ladies, and the pitch of laughter will increase noticeably. Although the best audience has an equal balance of men and women, given a choice of an all-male audience or one composed entirely of women, the professional humorist will choose the ladies.

If one or two people begin to laugh uproariously, you are off to a perfect start. The trick now is to keep them laughing.

When you start reeling off your opening stories, observe where the laughter is coming from. Look for the laughing women. Then pay special attention to those individuals. This does not mean that you should address all of your remarks to them but that you should certainly direct a few of your best lines to them.

It is always great fun to watch an expert at work. I remember observing an old friend of mine, a practiced after-dinner speaker, as he sized up his audience before delivering the principal address. During dinner, he looked out over the audience from his strategic position at the head table. He listened to the buzz of the crowd. He searched out the gayest and noisiest tables.

At a table near the front of the hall there was one particular woman who seemed to be the center of her small group. She was happy and loud. She appeared to laugh at the slightest provocation. My friend asked the man next to him who the lady was. "Oh," he said, "she is Evelyn------. Her husband is a past president of the association. She is a character. She likes a good time. Everybody knows her, and they all love her."

I knew my friend had a reason for asking about her. And sure enough, as he began feeling the response to his humor, he directed several of his best stories in her direction. After about five minutes she had become so hysterical that she suddenly began to laugh in the middle of his next story. Then he did it. He stopped in the middle of his story, leaned over the lectern and spoke directly to her in a loud stage whisper: "Not yet, Evelyn. Wait for the punch line."

Of course, Evelyn was taken off guard. She had no idea the speaker even knew her name. Instantly she became the center of attention of the entire room.

Her reaction? She exploded! She screamed and she howled.

Everyone at her table roared.

The whole room picked up the laughter for one full minute of bedlam.

That one remark made the evening for my friend. From then on he had that audience in the palm of his hand.

The only way to develop that kind of skill is by careful study and observation plus a bit of experience.

In like manner, experience is the only teacher of the tricks for dealing with distractions during a speech. Set rules cannot be given because no situation repeats itself in exactly the same way. Every new experience is just that—a new experience.

In coping with interruptions, if you want a rule to follow, it might be this: Don't fight back. Be gracious and polite. Give the appearance of enjoying your work. If you are doing a good job, your audience will regret the distraction even more than you do. Your listeners will be on your side, so don't try to squelch the distraction. Let your friends in the audience work on it for you.

Here is a case that illustrates my point. Once when a good friend of mine was speaking, I saw a hotel bellman enter the banquet hall with a telegram. He spoke to someone near the door and was directed to the head table. As he approached the head table the man on the end pointed toward the center. The bellman tiptoed behind the table to the toastmaster, who was seated to the right of the speaker.

It was tragic. All eyes were on the bellman as he made his way to the toastmaster. The speaker was rapidly losing the attention of the audience. But he was smart. He had attended many banquets and he guessed that the telegram was nothing more than a greeting from some celebrity. He stopped his speech and said to the toastmaster, "Oh, I see you have received a telegram. I'm sure everybody would like to know what it says. I wonder if you would please stand up and read it to them." The toastmaster read the message. The speaker had guessed correctly. The telegram was from the governor of the state saying he was sorry he could not be present and conveying his wishes for a successful convention.

The speaker led the applause for the reading.

Then he said to the audience, "I really didn't care whether or not the toastmaster read the telegram to you, but I was dying to know what was in it myself. Now I can get my mind back on what I was saying." What he really meant was that the audience could resume paying attention to what he was saying.

Sometimes a speaker must cope with people who continue to talk while the speaker is talking. At a meeting I attended one night in Washington, D.C., the speaker was interrupted several times by a man directly in front of the head table who was conversing with the man next to him. After about three minutes of trying to ignore the noise, the speaker stopped in the middle of his speech. He didn't say a word. He just stood there. Quietly waiting. Within a few seconds the man realized that his voice was the only voice in the room. His reaction was unexpected. Instead of keeping quiet, he said to the speaker,

"Do you want to hear what I'm saying?" And the speaker replied, calmly and politely, "No, not at all. But I do think most of the people in the room would like to hear what I have to say." And the audience burst into applause. The man stopped talking.

On another occasion I heard a speaker who was interrupted at least three or four times by a man who was quite inebriated. This fellow actually stood up in front of the podium and made remarks to the audience. The speaker was from out of town and did not know the man. He was extremely polite to him and always picked up the thread of his speech where it had been interrupted. It was a trying experience. After his address the speaker was congratulated for the way he handled the situation and thanked profusely by the chairman. It came out that the man creating the disturbance was a vice-president of the company and the guest of honor at the convention. No one, of course, dared to remove him.

For the best results try to ignore the distraction. Always appear to be calm and unruffled. Let the sympathy and goodwill of the audience help you weather the storm.

PRACTICE

The art of telling stories and making people laugh is similar to any other skill. You may understand the techniques of platform performance, but you'll never become a polished speaker without practice. The more you practice the greater your success will be.

There are, of course, a number of effective practice methods. Here are some suggested guidelines, which will *work for you* if you will *work at them.*

1. Select the story that you want to learn. Be convinced that you have chosen a funny story.

2. Write and rewrite the story in your own words—the

vocabulary that you use in everyday conversation. Write down the story as you would tell it if you were sitting and chatting with friends. Change any inappropriate words. For instance, if you want to use a story from a joke dictionary that talks about pounds and shillings, you will have to substitute dollars and cents to make the story suitable for an American audience.

3. Next, start practicing the story. Repeat it over and over again to yourself until you have it memorized word for word as you have it written down on paper. Repeat it aloud to yourself. Practice it while you are driving to work. Practice it during your coffee break. Practice every chance you get during the day.

4. Then record the story. Put it on tape. Put it on tape half a dozen times if necessary, one time after the other. Speak it and tell it—don't read it. Put all the dramatic emphasis into the story as you would do if you were standing before twelve hundred people. Then play the tapes back.

5. Criticize your own recordings. See if you have followed the rules. Be sure that your story is short and to the point and free of superfluous material. Check the composition of the story to be certain that you are telling it with the best possible choice of words. Rewrite it again if necessary.

6. Once you have the story down pat and are satisfied with the expression you are giving the words, practice the story in front of a mirror. This is the moment when you try out the facial expressions and hand and body movements you are going to use. After you have practiced them so that they seem natural, you are ready for the next step.

7. Tell the story to your friends. Every time you can gather an audience of even two people, tell them your story. At first you may find that some of your friends are

avoiding you, but don't give up. If you have the makings of a good storyteller, your friends will eventually come around. In time you will find people seeking you out to be entertained by your latest stories.

8. The next step is to move on to larger groups. Try your stories before groups of six or eight. Tell stories at parties, or become the unofficial storyteller of your own luncheon club. You will win your diploma as a storyteller the day when you are able to raise a belly laugh at the breakfast table from your wife and children. This is perhaps the final test. When you can accomplish this feat, you not only have a good story, but you have learned to tell it to perfection.

III
MAKE IT FIT

Humor must be relevant to your speech or else it won't succeed. Humor is like a suit of clothes. You might pay a top price for a suit made of the finest material, but you would look rather foolish wearing it if it were made for a six-foot-six basketball player and you were only five-foot-four.

In other words, you must tell the right story at the right place, at the right time and for the right purpose. Like a suit of clothes, humor must be tailor-made for the occasion.

Take your opener, for example. Searching for a laugh-getter, you find this story in a book: "A service club in Denver used to grade its guest speakers. A standing ovation won four bells, an excellent speech won three bells. An average speaker was given two bells and a poor one received one bell. They had one speaker who was awarded the no-bell prize."

The wrong way to lead into that story is: "As I stand here, I am reminded of a story about a service club in Denver that had a unique way of grading guest speakers. . . ."

Here's the way to make that story fit your speech. "I want to thank Mr. Program Chairman for that eloquent introduction. I wish I could speak as well as he can. There is a service club in Harrisburg (name a city that is well-known to the audience and in the same state) that grades its guest speakers by printing little bells after the review of their speeches in the club bulletin. They give four bells to the speakers who get standing ovations. Three bells go to those that are rated excellent. Average speakers get two bells and the poor ones are given one bell. I spoke there three weeks ago. That's the day I was awarded the no-bell prize."

Here is another opener as it appeared in a book:

A Baltimore newspaperman was invited to speak at a Chamber of Commerce meeting in a small Texas town. He was almost frightened to death when he noticed that most of the men in the audience were wearing six-shooters. His fears increased after he had finished speaking and sat down, because one of the men drew his guns and rushed toward the head table. "Don't be afraid of him," the president of the club said. "He's not going to bother you. He's after the man who introduced you."

That story is a great laugh getter, but it won't create a ripple if you tell it as it was printed in the book. Again, it's like a suit of clothes—good material, but it needs a few alterations to make it fit.

How do you make that story fit your speech if you are addressing a group of insurance salesmen in the auditorium of the schoolhouse in Effingham, Illinois? To begin with, think about your audience and the place where you are telling the story. Your audience couldn't care less about a newspaperman from Baltimore. They came to hear you, so why not tell them something about yourself:

I hope this meeting tonight doesn't end up like the one where I spoke not long ago. It was in Texas. I was speaking to a group of ranchers in the high school auditorium. [This sounds like a true story.] As the auditorium began to fill up, I noticed that most of the men were wearing pistols. This was the first time I had ever spoken in Texas and I was scared to death. But I had to make my speech, and I went right ahead with it. After I had been talking for about two minutes, one of the men in the front row jumped up, drew both of his guns and began to take aim at the head table. [Pull out two imaginary pistols and take aim.] That's when I stopped. I turned to the president of the association and said: "What's wrong? What did I say to offend that fellow?" And the president said, "Oh, don't pay any attention to him. He's not going to hurt you. But I sure do pity the fellow who introduced you."

If you are looking for a closer instead of an opener, that same story can be altered to serve as the conclusion of your speech: "Before I sit down, I want to say that I hope this meeting doesn't end up like the one where I spoke. . . ."

If you use a little imagination you can adapt practically any story to your needs. With a funny punch line on the tip of your tongue you can rework a story to make it suit any occasion. Don't be afraid to twist a story around to make it timely. If you want to use a Hitler-Goebbels story that you found in an old joke book, substitute two contemporary political figures and you may have a big laugh getter.

With some slight modifications you can make your story move effortlessly from Los Angeles to Tulsa to Tampa, to fit the occasion.

I have a friend who really uses his ingenuity. He's funny. I've laughed at him many times, although I have heard him tell only one story in public. He's a genius with that one story. He can twist it around to fit any occasion. And he always gets a laugh with it.

The first time I heard him tell the story was at a service club meeting where he had been asked to speak for five minutes on his occupation. This is how he told the story to fit that occasion:

The other day my twelve-year-old daughter went to the library and said to the librarian, "I want to learn something about the Nile River for school. Can you help me, please?" The librarian said she would be glad to help. After about twenty minutes she had assembled a stack of books about two feet high. "There," she said, "that will tell you all about the Nile River." My daughter stood and looked at the stack of books and said, "I certainly do thank you for all of your trouble, but I don't want to know that much about the Nile River." I have been asked to tell you about my business. I could talk all afternoon about my company, but I am sure you are like my little girl. You don't want to know that much about it. So for the next five minutes I'll . . .

Some weeks later I was attending a PTA meeting and he was in the audience. As it so often happens, a controversial subject had come up and it was being talked to death. Everybody was tired of discussing it, and the meeting was dragging on and on. Finally my friend stood up and was recognized by the chair. He told the story about his little girl and then said, ". . . and I think all of us have heard all we want to hear about the subject. I would like to vote on it. I call for a motion." It worked. It worked because he made a funny story fit the time, the place and his purpose.

I heard him tell that same story again when several of us were attending a citizens' association meeting. It was apparent that a small group was trying to rush through a resolution without allowing a full discussion of the subject. My friend stood up and told his story and then said, "I'm like my daughter. I don't want to know all there is to know about the subject, but I certainly do want to know more about it than I have heard thus far. And I am sure there are others who feel as I do. I have a couple of questions. . . ."

I thought I had heard the last of the story until about six months later, when he was speaking at a state convention of his own trade association. His topic concerned a piece of legislation under consideration. He opened his speech with his story and then he said: "Too many people are like that little girl. They want to know as little as they can in order to get by in this world. I am glad you are not like that. I am happy and pleased that you have invited me to come here and to discuss . . ."

I'm looking forward to hearing him speak again one of these days.

The following examples will show you how to fit a story to your speech:

Necessity for spending more money. You are presiding over a meeting where some serious problems must be resolved and you know that the solutions will cost money. You prepare your audience by telling them: "A fellow where I work went home the other evening and found his wife crying. Being a man of much experience, he didn't say anything to her. After he had taken off his hat and coat she said, 'You don't love me anymore. You come home and find me crying and you don't even ask me what's the matter.' 'I'm sorry, honey,' he said, 'but every time I ask you what's the matter, it ends up costing me money.' Tonight we are gathered here to ask, 'What's the matter?' and I'm afraid the necessary remedies will cost us some money."

Wise spending. You want to illustrate the point that bargain buying is sometimes deceptive. "I was chatting with a friend the other day and I mentioned that my son's seventeenth birthday was coming up. If I bought him what he had asked for I was going to be out two hundred dollars. And my friend said, 'Well, that's one thing you can say for my boy. He was seventeen three months ago and the gift he asked for cost me only seventy-five cents.' I couldn't understand how my friend could get off that easily, so I said, 'What in the world could you buy today for only seventy-five cents that would satisfy any normal seventeen-year-old boy?' 'Oh,' he said, 'that was easy. I gave him his own set of keys to the car.' Let's not be like that man. Let's not fool ourselves. When we begin to consider our budget for this year, let's look . . ."

Things are not as bad as they seem. You are speaking at a trade association meeting. "When I was a boy, we had a neighbor who was a hypochondriac. She had been pestering all of the doctors in town for years. Nobody could please her. Then one day a new doctor moved into town. He was just out of medical school. She was one of his first patients. 'I have heart trouble,' she told him. Then she spent about an hour describing all of her symptoms and ended by asking him, 'I do have heart trouble, don't

I?' 'Not necessarily,' he said. 'With the symptoms you have described to me, you might have something much less serious.' She jumped out of the chair and said, 'Huh, you're a smart young whippersnapper. Why, you're just out of school. You have nerve, disagreeing with an experienced invalid like me.' I'm afraid we have a great many people in our association who think our situation is worse than it actually is. . . ."

Facing up to problems. You want to urge your listeners to face a problem honestly. This story will dramatize your point. "I had a friend who went to see his doctor. He said to the doctor, 'I want you to give me a thorough examination and then tell me in plain words what's the matter with me. I don't want any of those fancy medical terms. Just tell me in plain language.' The doctor gave him a complete physical and then told him his trouble. 'There's nothing wrong with you,' the doctor said. 'You're just lazy. Plain lazy.' My friend looked at the doctor and said, 'Now, if you don't mind, please give me the fancy medical terms for it so I can tell my wife.' Tonight I think we should quit kidding ourselves. I think we should tell it like it is. And that is what I am going to do."

Stimulating action. You are trying to get members of your service club to get to work. "I had an uncle who was a farmer. His crops weren't flourishing, and the county agent was talking to him and trying to give him some new ideas. 'Onions are going to bring a good price this year and you have some mighty good onion land. You'd have no trouble getting the seed onions. What do you think of that?' 'Oh, the idea's all right, I guess,' my uncle said, 'but even if I got the onion seed, my old woman's too blamed lazy to do the plowing and planting.' And that's the trouble with a lot of us. We complain because the other fellow is too lazy to do our work for us."

Stay alert. Twist this story around when you want to

show that any problem can be solved if you are alert for the answer. "When I was a boy we lived in a tourist town. During the winter when we went to church, half of the congregation were visitors and strangers. I'll never forget one Sunday. The strangest thing happened. Our minister preached only five minutes. When he finished his sermon he explained why. 'I'm sorry to cut my sermon so short this morning,' he said. 'But while I was having breakfast our dog came into my study and chewed up my sermon notes and left me with only one page.' After church was over and the people were shaking hands with the minister, one of the out-of-town visitors said to him, 'I was just wondering if that dog of yours has any pups. I'd like to take one back home with me and give it to our minister.' Now, there was a man who knew an opportunity when he saw one."

Trying new ideas. Here is a story that will impress your audience with the possibility of applying new ideas and solutions to old problems. "My neighbor has a little eight-year-old girl. The other day she brought home her report card from school. She had several A's and a couple of B's. A fine report card, but the teacher had written across the bottom, 'Mary Ann is a smart little girl. She has only one fault. She talks too much in school. I have a system I am going to try, which I think may break her of the habit.' My friend signed the report card for Mary Ann and then wrote just below the teacher's note. He said, 'Please let me know if your system works on Mary Ann. I would like to try it on her mother.'"

The direct approach. When you want to use the direct approach to the topic of your speech you might begin this way: "The other evening I overheard my little boy talking to the kid next door. They were playing in the recreation room and didn't know the door was open. We had just given my little boy a puppy, and the kid next door was complaining to him because his folks wouldn't allow him to have a dog. 'They won't let me have a puppy,' he said. 'I've begged and begged and they always say no.' And my boy said to him, 'You just didn't go about it in the right way. You keep asking for a puppy. The best way to get a puppy is to beg for a baby brother—and they'll settle for a puppy every time.' He must have learned that technique from his mother, because I believe in getting straight to the point. And that is what I am going to do tonight, get straight to the point."

On the difficulty of communicating. You want to stress the point that communication, even within a group with similar aims, is often difficult. "Several months ago our local church purchased a set of electronic chimes, the kind that work from a tape with speakers that have adjustable volume control. Our plan was to mount the speakers in the steeple of the church and play sacred music every Sunday afternoon. In order to make sure we were not playing the chimes too loud for the neighbors, we sent out several teams of church members to the surrounding area to check on the volume level during our first concert. One of our deacons rang a doorbell, and the lady of the house came to the door. Our man said, 'I'm here from the . . .' 'What did you say?' the woman asked. Our man said, 'I said I am here from the church . . .' 'What did you say?' the lady asked. Our man was now shouting. 'I said I am here from the church to ask you . . .' And the lady shouted back at him, 'You'll have to talk louder. I can't hear a word you're saying on account of those darn chimes.' If we are going to communicate so that we all can understand, we must get rid of the extraneous noise and talk quietly about our problem."

Making yourself understood. You may be invited to speak on your specialty to an audience that is not familiar with the fundamentals of the subject. You want members of the audience to feel free to ask questions if they do not understand any portion of your speech. You tell them: "Sometimes we get so involved in our own specialty that we assume other people know more about it than they actually do. Last summer, my little five-year-old nephew was visiting us. When we took our children to Sunday school we put him in the class with the other five-year-olds. His teacher opened the lesson by saying, 'Today we are going to study about Peter. Can anybody tell me who Peter was?' My little nephew raised his hand, and the teacher said, 'Oh, this is nice. Our new little friend knows. Will you please stand up and tell all the other children—who was Peter?' And my little nephew said rather proudly, 'I fink he was a wabbit.' I don't want to start talking about things you don't understand, so if you have any questions as we go along, please don't hesitate to interrupt me."

Be calm and reasonable. When an emergency meeting has been convened, you may be called upon to urge the group to be calm and reasonable in its deliberations. You can use this story to illustrate your message: "The other day I was watching a father minding a baby in front of the supermarket. The baby was in his carriage and he was screaming his head off. The father was leaning over the carriage and patting the baby tenderly. I couldn't help overhear what he was saying: 'There, there, Wilbur, take it easy. It's not as bad as it seems, Wilbur. Mommy will be out of the store in a few minutes. Just don't panic, Wilbur. Now, Wilbur, keep calm. Everything is going to be all right. Remember, Wilbur, this whole unpleasant experience is going to be over in another few minutes.' I wasn't the only one watching the doting father. A woman had been standing there waiting for her husband to bring their car around, and she thought she'd help the man. She leaned over the carriage and said to the baby, 'Now, Wilbur, don't cry anymore. Your daddy is going to look after you. Everything is going to be all right.' And right then I thought the man was going to burst into tears as he said to the lady, 'Look, lady, his name is Charlie. I'm Wilbur.' So before we begin discussing this thorny problem tonight, I'd suggest that all of us determine to be calm and not get overwrought. In that way I am sure we'll be able to work out a proper solution."

Acting without due deliberation. You may want to point out that no decision should be made too quickly. "A man went to see his lawyer and said to him, 'I want to get a divorce. My wife hasn't spoken to me for three months.' The lawyer said to him, 'If I were you, I'd think about that for a while. Don't be too hasty. Wives like that are mighty hard to find these days.' I think we should postpone this question until more of us have had time to think about it."

On being unreasonable. You are trying to convince your audience not to adopt a frivolous or superficial plan. "About a year ago I was invited to speak to a women's group in our town. They gave me about four weeks notice and suggested that I speak on the subject of 'The Early Art of the Ming Dynasty.' I didn't know anything about Chinese art, much less about the art of the Ming Dynasty, and I had to spend about ten or twelve nights boning up on it. On the day of the speech I arrived on time for the luncheon and I have never been treated more graciously. My hostess told me, 'We're so glad you could be with us on this special occasion. And we think it is wonderful that you are going to talk to us about Chinese art. You see, it ties in with our theme for today. We're having chow mein for lunch.' Let's be a little more sensible in our planning than those women were. . . ."

Making mountains out of molehills. You want to make the point that the members of the organization are letting their imaginations run away with them over a minor, insignificant matter. This story will serve your purpose: "Several weeks ago when I was coming home from a trip, I had the aisle seat in a row of three seats on the airplane. About half an hour before we were scheduled to land, the young man sitting next to the window turned and said to the man sitting between us, 'Excuse me, sir, would you lend me your cigarette lighter, please?' The man in the middle was old enough to be the young fellow's father. He sat for a moment looking at the young man and then he said, 'No, I won't let you borrow my lighter. Because if I let you borrow my lighter, we'll probably strike up a conversation. And by the time we land we'll be so interested in becoming acquainted that I'll ask you to have a drink in the bar until my family comes to meet me. Then, when they arrive, I would introduce you to my wife. And, just to be friendly, she might ask you to come to the house for dinner. You probably would accept. Then, when we got home for dinner, you would meet my twenty-year-old daughter. After dinner we would sit around and chat and she would probably invite you to come again. After that whenever you came to town you would call on my daughter. And a romance would be sure to blossom. Someday you would want to marry that lovely child. And I wouldn't stand for it. I don't want my daughter marrying anybody who is too stupid to carry a cigarette lighter.' It seems to me that some of the arguments tonight are being built up from the same kind of small beginning."

When there are two points of view. You want to illustrate the fact that there are two ways of looking at the question under discussion. "There are two ways to look at this question. Like the two young ladies who were talking about a wealthy bachelor. 'He's rich,' said the first girl. 'I know that, but he's too old to be eligible.' 'No, he isn't,' her friend said. 'I think he's too eligible to be old.' So let's take a lesson from those young ladies and look at both sides of this question."

When there are only two choices. You want to make the point that there are only two choices. "A man was consulting his lawyer and said, 'Isn't there some way that a man can keep from having to pay alimony?' 'Yes,' his lawyer said. 'He can either stay single or stay married.' So it seems to me that we have two choices here tonight. We can either . . ."

Making excuses. At one time or another every speaker finds himself having to say a word or two about people who make excuses—excuses for not paying dues, excuses for not attending meetings, excuses for leaving before meetings are over, etc. The following stories can be altered to fit any "excuse" occasion. "I sneaked off one Sunday and went fishing with a friend of mine. We weren't catching anything and were feeling a bit guilty about it and I said to him, 'I guess we should have gone to church instead of coming out to the lake.' 'Oh,' he said, 'I couldn't have gone to church today. My wife is sick in bed.' And most excuses sound just that silly."

Or: "A friend of mine went next door and asked his neighbor if he could borrow his power lawn mower. 'I'm sorry,' the neighbor said, 'I can't let you have it. My daughter is getting married next Thursday down in Biloxi, Mississippi.' 'What's that got to do with you lending me your lawn mower? That's no excuse for not lending me your lawn mower for an hour.' 'Listen,' his neighbor said, 'if I don't want to lend you my lawn mower, any excuse is good enough.' And so it is in our association. If we don't want to . . ."

The attractive package. You are introducing a new

saying, "My friend, the speaker, is like the new preacher who moved to town when I was a boy. For the first six weeks he preached a series of sermons on sin. He really let the people in town have the last word on the subject. One day after church a neighbor of ours told him, 'My, you are a powerful preacher. Why, we didn't know what sin was until you moved to town.' And you folks today don't know what this subject is all about until you have heard Mr. Speaker."

Apologize for overcrowding. You are the program chairman and are faced with an overflow crowd in the dining room. While the management is setting up additional seats you want to make sure that the audience accepts the situation with good humor. Here is a story to tell: "My daughter's boyfriend was telling her about his new car. 'It sounds wonderful,' she said. 'How many will it hold?' 'Well,' he said, 'it's built to hold four, but you can get six in it if they are well acquainted and friendly.' I am sure that all of us are well enough acquainted to enjoy a little crowding tonight. . . ."

When things are running late. It is not unusual for banquets to run behind schedule. You can adjust this story to fit the circumstances. "A friend of mine is the head of an advertising firm on Madison Avenue. Some of his employees live in New Jersey and commute to work. Last winter, during the big blizzard, one of the commuter trains was caught in the snowdrifts, and everyone on board was stranded overnight. By the middle of the following morning, one of my friend's employees who was on board the train managed to make his way to the depot and send this telegram to the office: 'Sorry, I won't be at work today. Not home from work yesterday yet.' It looks as though we are running a little behind schedule with our program tonight, but I assure you we are going to let you get home sometime tonight."

When you are hoarse. Now that speakers have public address systems at their disposal, they no longer need to raise their voices or shout. Even though the pitcher of water on the lectern may no longer be a necessity, there are times, however, when a sudden hoarse throat makes you want to have a glass of water handy. The situation itself is good for a laugh: "I appreciate the thoughtfulness of the chairman for this glass of water." (Pick it up and hold it for all to see.) "I remember the first speech I ever made years ago. I was scared to death. I was afraid nobody would applaud my oratory or laugh at my funny stories. Just to be on the safe side, I had my best friend come to the meeting with me. I asked him to sit down front and applaud and laugh at me. I told him that when I wiped my forehead with my handkerchief he was supposed to laugh and when I stopped to take a sip of water, he should applaud. He said, 'Sure, I'll be there. But you'd better switch those signals, because I'll just naturally laugh out loud every time I see you taking a sip of water.' So if you see me take a sip of water tonight, you don't have to laugh. I'm taking it because my throat is a bit hoarse."

Remember what we said earlier. Fitting humor to your speech is like a tailor fitting a new suit to you. It requires a great deal of care in selecting the proper material. It takes work and patience to trim the material and lay the pieces in order. And it takes skill to put the pieces together. The secret of success for a storyteller is the same as it is for the tailor: first master the techniques and then practice, practice, practice.

IV
LAUGH-GETTING OPENERS

This chapter provides helpful pointers on how to get your speech off to a fast start. Also included are examples of time-tested, surefire, laugh-getting openers that you can modify and adjust to suit your own speech.

YOUR INTRODUCTION

Your introduction is the most important single factor in getting your speech started in high gear. Nothing in your introduction should be left to chance or to the whim of the program chairman.

After accepting a speaking engagement, your first step should be to send a copy of your introduction to the program chairman. Better yet, send him two copies. One copy is for him to use when he introduces you and the other copy is for him to misplace or lose in his files. To make sure that nothing will go wrong, always have an extra copy in your pocket when you arrive at the appointed place of your speaking engagement.

This important piece of paper should be written word for word the way you want to be introduced. Don't send the program chairman a biographical sketch and expect him to extract the pertinent facts and write an introduction that will get you off to a dramatic start. This is your introduction. Give it to the program chairman exactly as you want to be presented.

Giving the program chairman a prepared introduction will make his work easier for him. He will appreciate your thoughtfulness. More important, you will be presented to the audience in an ideal manner. Also, if you know exactly what the program chairman is going to say, you can have a carefully rehearsed response, including a funny story that will tie in with the introduction.

Your introduction should be concise and to the point. Provide enough background material to establish you as an authority on your subject. However, don't overdo it. If you are speaking to a group of engineers and you have an engineering degree, by all means mention it. But don't deluge the audience with extraneous facts—for example, your lodge affiliations or the names and ages of your children.

On the other hand, if you are speaking to a lodge and you are a member of the same order, be sure to mention it. That fact is of greater interest to that audience than your academic background.

Here is a sample introduction which I have used many times. You will notice that there is a place where a few sentences or remarks germane to the particular local situation can be inserted.

Our speaker is Winston K. Pendleton of Windermere,

Florida. Mr. Pendleton is a former newspaperman and public relations consultant. He is a retired vice-president and sales manager of the Universal Dynamics Corporation. He is a nationally known public speaker and writer and is the author of three best sellers. His latest book is entitled *Aw Stop Worryin'*.

[INSERT CAN BE MADE HERE.]

During his years in Washington, where so many of the answers to vital world problems are hammered out, Mr. Pendleton developed a keen understanding of people and the tensions under which they work. He is going to talk to us about some of the problems of mental stress and strain. He is going to give us his ideas about how to cure the worry habit.

It is my pleasure to present Winston K. Pendleton. The title of his address is the same as that of his newest book: "Aw Stop Worryin'."

This introduction can be used for any group, with an insert to tie in with the particular audience. For example, when I speak to a Rotary meeting, these lines are inserted: "In making this introduction, I am going to refer to our speaker as Win because he is a fellow Rotarian. He is a member of the Rotary Club of Windermere, Florida. He is a past District Governor of District 760, which covers eastern Virginia."

For a church group, such as a family-night dinner or the annual banquet of the "Men of the Church," the following paragraph can be added to help build rapport with the audience: "Mr. Pendleton has more than fifteen years of experience as the teacher of an adult Bible class. He is a member of the First Christian Church of Ocoee, Florida."

If you have been invited to speak at a county-wide

44

meeting following an earlier appearance at the state convention of the same organization, this insert would be appropriate: "Last spring, Mr. Pendleton spoke to our state convention in Atlanta. Those of us who heard him that night thought so much of his message that we have prevailed on him to come here tonight for our annual meeting."

Regardless of how you write it, be sure that the man who is to introduce you has been given a prepared introduction. The importance of having the right kind of introduction cannot be overemphasized. Many a speech has started awkwardly because something was either omitted from or added to an introduction which threw the speaker off guard.

The first thirty seconds following the introduction can be the most critical thirty seconds of the speech. During those few seconds, the speaker has the rapt attention of the audience. There is a natural air of expectancy in the room as he steps to the lectern.

If he is ready with his first sentence, if he is full of confidence, if he is able to move off instantly like a well-trained soldier stepping off to the first beat of the drum, he will be off to a strong start.

On the other hand, if the toastmaster has said something to dumbfound or confuse the speaker, the speaker's discomfiture will show on his face as he steps to the microphone. Moreover, if the toastmaster has used an impromptu funny story to introduce the speaker, the audience expects the speaker to have a humorous reply. With only five seconds to think of one, the speaker is at a definite disadvantage. This sort of situation can upset any speaker. He may recover if he is a man of experience, but his job is certainly made more difficult than it need be.

Let us suppose that you are a highly regarded physician

from out of the city. You have come to speak to a cross section of citizens on a serious subject. Imagine what would happen if the local toastmaster, attempting to make a humorous introduction, concluded with this remark: "And so, ladies and gentlemen, I am proud to introduce to you Dr. Johnston. Dr. Johnston is the doctor who treated an uncle of mine following a serious illness. A number of doctors said that my uncle would never be able to walk again, but Dr. Johnston said he would have him back on his feet in six weeks. And he did. When he sent his bill to my uncle, my uncle had to sell his car. Ladies and gentlemen, Dr. Johnston."

Now, if Dr. Johnston possesses an amazing sense of humor and has a vast repertoire of stories, he might be able to step to the microphone and say: "Yes, I remember your uncle well. He was suffering from an arrested case of severe alcoholitis intoxicantis. In layman's language that means your uncle was put in jail for being drunk."

But how many speakers can always come up with a sharp retort while they are thinking nervously about their opening remarks? Very few. There is only one safe way to be sure of winning an audience with a bit of clever repartee. Have the straight lines written into your introduction and your clever reply carefully rehearsed.

Balance is a necessary element in a good introduction. If you have given the toastmaster too much information, his introduction might easily become a long-winded speech. If the toastmaster happens to be a poor speaker, he will bore the audience. If the audience has become restless before you start your speech, you will have an uphill struggle to regain their interest.

Also, there is such a thing as a too short introduction. The worst introduction I ever heard given, and perhaps the rudest, was at a banquet at which the president of the club stood up and said, "A few moments ago someone told me that I was to have the job of introducing our speaker tonight. Well, ladies and gentlemen, here he is." It so happened that the speaker that night was a man with a quick mind who had a great deal of platform experience. Like a champion pitcher fielding a hot line drive, he said, "I want to thank President Harris for that gracious introduction. And since I am a bit of an egomaniac, I would like to make a few additional remarks about myself. My name is Jack Jackson and I . . ." He then carefully presented the parts of his background that were relevant to the topic of his speech.

To make absolutely certain that your audience is handed over to you in the best possible condition, quiet and eager to hear your first words, have a carefully prepared introduction for the man who has been assigned the job of presenting you. In that way you can always be sure that your opening remarks will relate to and mesh with your introduction.

SOME LAUGH-GETTING OPENERS

Referring to your introduction is always good for a laugh. If the program chairman reads your prepared introduction, you might open by saying, "I want to thank my good friend for that gracious introduction. He read it exactly the way I wrote it." If this is said with the proper inflection and a bow to the chairman, it will get a laugh. Follow up that laugh with: "Well, that's important. Some of these fellows who don't often get a chance at the speaker's stand sometimes try to use up all of the guest speaker's time by making a long-winded speech. Three weeks ago I was speaking to an oil dealers' convention in Cincinnati. The man who introduced me took thirty-five minutes. He forgot I was even in the room." (Look at the chair where you were seated—good for a small laugh.) "Finally he remembered what he was supposed to be doing, and he tried to make it up to me by really buttering me up. He concluded his remarks by introducing me as the man who had just made $800,000 in an oil deal in Oklahoma. Of course, that wasn't true. It wasn't an oil deal—it was a real estate deal." (Some people in the audience will think that is the end of the story and they will laugh; let them.) "And it wasn't in Oklahoma, it was in Florida. And he got his figures all mixed up. It wasn't $800,000, it was $800." This will get a laugh. "And besides, it wasn't a profit, it was a loss." Remember, this is your punch line. You should practice it well. If you say it with a look of disappointment on your face, you'll get the kind of opening laugh you want.

Here are two openers to follow your prepared introduction:

Thank you, Mr. Chairman, for that fine introduction. With those kind words, I certainly am off to a good start. But that doesn't indicate how this speech might end.

[1] After I had spoken last week at a big dinner meeting, I was milling around with the crowd as they were going out the door and I overheard a woman talking to her husband. "Oh, that speaker tonight. I'm so full of his message that I can hardly speak." And her husband said, "I know exactly how you feel. I got a bellyful of him myself."

[2] Two weeks ago I spoke at a banquet in Richmond. After the dinner was over, I was standing with the president of the association at the door of the dining room and shaking hands with people as they were leaving. I never received so many compliments in my life. One man even called my speech an oration. Another shook hands with me and said, "That was a great speech. I could have listened to you for another hour

and a half." [Here you will get an extra laugh.] Then
the last man wandered out. He shook my hand and
said, "I thought it stunk." I told him that I didn't quite
understand what he meant. "You ought to. I said it
plain enough. That was the worst speech ever given
at one of these meetings and whoever invited you to
speak ought to be put out of the association." He went
on out. The president, of course, was terribly embarrassed. He said, "Don't pay any attention to that fellow.
He's a half-wit. Why, that man has never had an original idea in his life. All he does is stand around and
listen to what other people say and then he goes
around repeating it."

After a strong introduction, you might use one of the
following approaches:

Thank you for that flattering introduction. About the
only thing you didn't say about me is that I was born
in a log cabin. No, I wasn't born in a log cabin, but I
do want to say this: my folks moved into one just as
soon as they could afford it.

As I was being introduced, I was sitting here thinking about the three hardest things in the world to do.
The first is to climb over a barbed-wire fence when it
is leaning toward you. The second is to kiss a pretty girl
when she is leaning away from you. And the third is to
try to live up to that flattering introduction just given
to me by the chairman.

One time there was a judge trying a divorce case. He
had never had a case like this one. The woman had
been married only one day. He was questioning her
about her problem. "I can't understand why you want
a divorce. You married the most eligible man in town.
He was the best-looking man in town. He was rich. He

didn't smoke. He didn't drink. He didn't run around. All of your friends had been telling you those things about him for years. Then you married him yesterday and today you want a divorce. I can't understand it. What's your problem anyway?" "Well, judge, I guess that's my problem. The man was just naturally over-introduced."

If you are from a small town, the following routine will provoke a lot of laughter and get your speech off to a jolly start. However, if you are going to use this approach, you must have some lines written into your introduction that will set the stage, such as: "Our speaker is from Berryville. Of course, I never heard of Berryville, but I suppose there is such a place because our speaker is here and he says that's where he is from."

With that introduction, you can use your jokes about Berryville, or any other small town. You may want to write your own routine about a small town. The following one can serve as a model.

When the chairman introduced me he said he had never heard of Berryville. Maybe Berryville isn't famous, but it is a delightful place to live in and we are proud of our town. You all know what a small town is. That's where everybody knows what everybody else is doing, but they read the weekly newspaper to see if they've been caught at it. [Watch your timing after each of these lines.] We have 115 registered voters. We have a mayor and a city council. They are a wide-awake bunch of fellows. Last summer some kids were stealing hub caps around town. We don't want any juvenile delinquency in our town so the city council passed a curfew. After three nights they had to repeal it. Because every night when they blew the whistle at nine o'clock, it woke up everybody.

We do keep up-to-date, though. We had a traffic jam one day, so the city council voted to put in one-way streets. We only have one street. That day when everybody drove out of town, nobody could get back home for supper.

I will admit that we are a bit isolated. Last year during the hurricane we were cut off from the rest of the state for four days. And it was three days before anybody realized it. I guess we are rather small compared to other towns. Our Howard Johnson has only one flavor of ice cream, and our phone book has only one yellow page. But we do have some excitement now and then. Last summer the packing house burned down. It caught fire about nine o'clock at night. Ordinarily it would have burned down in about an hour. But we have a volunteer fire department, and they arrived in about ten minutes. They're pretty good. They were able to keep that fire going until three o'clock in the morning. Whether you are from a small town as I am or from one of the great cities of America, you cannot help but be concerned about the problems of . . . And so into your speech.

Here are some lines that can be inserted into your introduction which will get a big laugh. Have your introduction end with these words: "It warms the cockles of my heart to present at this time------, who will speak on the subject of------" Your opening laugh will come when you say, "It made me happy when Mr. Chairman said that my being here warmed the cockles of his heart, because I would hate to think of him sitting at the head table all evening with a heart full of cold cockles."

If the chairman has called you an expert when he introduced you, try this one. "Mr. Chairman called me an expert. I've often heard that an expert is anyone with an attaché case in his hand and fifty miles away from home. And my teen-age daughter says that an expert is like the bottom of a double boiler—throws off a lot of steam, but never really knows what's cooking."

Another opening approach: As soon as you step up to the microphone to speak, touch it lightly and appear to jiggle it a bit, and then say, "I'm glad this thing is steady. The other night I was introduced to speak and as I stepped up to the platform the microphone kept dropping down. I pushed it up, but it fell back. After I had done that about four times, the man who had introduced me jumped up to fix it. He said, 'Folks, don't worry. Nothing's the matter except I think our speaker has a screw loose.'"

If you step up to the microphone and find that it is not properly adjusted for your height or stance, go ahead and adjust it. While you are fixing it, you can say: "Can you hear me back there? Now can you hear me? The other night I was speaking and right in the middle of my speech the public address system went dead. I tried to talk without it, but I noticed a fellow in the back with his hand up to his ear" (put your hand up to your ear) "straining to hear me. He said, 'Louder.' I raised my voice, but he kept saying, 'Louder.' I kept raising my voice until I was shouting at him." (As you tell this story, gradually raise your voice until you are shouting.) "Finally, I was shouting so loud that it bothered a man sitting down front. He couldn't stand all the noise. He jumped up and yelled at the man in the back." You now cup your hands and shout at the back of the auditorium. "'What's the matter back there, can't you hear him?' The man in the back said, 'No, not a word.' And that fellow down front shouted, 'Well, move over buddy, I'm coming back to sit with you.'"

After the chairman has introduced a speaker he may

suggest that everyone in the audience turn his chair around so he can see the speaker. You can follow up that remark by saying, "I hope everyone is comfortable now. But not too comfortable. I don't want you to be so comfortable that you go to sleep." (This should get anything from a chuckle to a hearty laugh, depending on how well you put it across.) "When I was speaking the other night a fellow did go to sleep. He got comfortable. He moved the dishes out of the way, put his arms down on the table and took a nap. It embarrassed his wife. I saw her trying to kick his foot under the table, but she couldn't reach that far. Finally she picked up a spoon and hit him over the head with it." (Have a spoon handy that you can grab and swing in the air as though you are hitting somebody on the head.) "That woke him up. He sat up, rubbed his head and said, 'Honey, you're going to have to hit me harder than that. I can still hear him.'"

When you are invited to speak to a service club that is not the one you belong to, here is a story that will bring down the house. You will have to practice it carefully in order not to get your words twisted. Let us say that you, a member of the Kiwanis Club, are invited to speak at a Lions Club charter night. Make sure that the chairman mentions that you are a Kiwanian when he introduces you. Then use this opener:

I'm happy that you Lions would invite a Kiwanian to speak tonight. This happens more often than you might imagine. Not long ago I was invited to speak to a big interclub meeting where the Lions and the Kiwanians and the Rotarians were all gathered together. After the meeting was over the presidents of the three clubs were chatting with me over a cup of coffee. The president of the Rotary Club said to the president of the Kiwanis Club, "I have always admired the work that you fellows do in this town, and if I were not a Rotarian I would be a Kiwanian." The president of the Kiwanis Club said the same thing: "If I weren't a Kiwanian, I'd be a Rotarian." I looked at the Lion. He was sitting there looking rather forlorn and I said to him, "You're a Lion. If you weren't a Lion, what would you be?" He looked at me and said, "If I weren't a Lion, I'd be a . . . shamed of myself." [This story takes practice. The punch line must be spoken as a single statement, but the word "ashamed" should be pronounced as though it were two words, like "a boat" or "a man."]

The occasion may arise when every facet of your background, even the most insignificant area, is mention by the chairman in his introduction. Every degree you have earned, every job you have held, every community and civic position you have served in is included. When this happens, you can lean over toward the man who has introduced you and say, "I'd like to see the sheet of paper that Mr. Chairman was reading from. I listened carefully to everything he said and I am sure he left something out. I recall that somewhere in my past I was also a newspaper boy." Or head of the Beaver Patrol in the Boy Scouts, or manager of the grammar school tiddlywinks team and so on.

Or, "I want to thank Mr. Chairman for that gracious introduction. I'm glad he didn't present me like a fellow in Pittsburgh did the other evening. He spoke at length about my background and accomplishments in Washington and praised the speech I was about to give and then said, 'So let's all of us relax and listen to the dope from Washington.'"

If a photographer takes your picture when you get up to speak, you might say, "Thanks for shooting my picture now. The other night in Dallas the photographer waited until my speech was over, and then he assembled some of the principals at the head table for a picture. The chairman was disturbed over the time he was taking and said, 'You should have shot the speaker before he spoke. That would have been much better.'"

Of all the many ways of leading into a funny story at the opening of a speech, the oldest is the show business classic—relating something that happened to you on the way to the meeting. Don't be corny about it and say, "A funny thing happened on the way to . . ." Follow the rule we gave you earlier and tell the story with utmost conviction, as though it had really happened to you. (Remember, you will have to have all of the towns and locations correctly placed for the story to ring true.)

You'll never know how happy I am to be standing here at this moment. I almost didn't make it. As I drove through Columbus on the way here, I stopped my car at a stoplight and afterward I couldn't get it to move. I blocked traffic and had an awful time. Finally a wrecker towed me to a garage, where they told me my transmission was shot and that my car wouldn't be repaired until the next day. I was desperate, so I took a taxi to the bus station and rushed in and asked the man at the ticket counter, "When's the next bus to Mansfield?" "You mean the last bus, buddy. It's out on the platform with its engine running and if you don't hurry, you'll miss it." I rushed out on the platform. There were about eight buses with their engines running and I got on the wrong bus. [You'll get a middle-of-the-story laugh if you say that line with a dejected expression on your face.] I got on a charter bus. It was going to Toledo, to the Ohio State Mental Hospital. It was filled with inmates, but I didn't know it. There was an empty seat so I sat down. And pretty soon a man came in checking his load. He began to count. "One, two, three, four, five, si . . . Who are you and where do you think you are going?" [This story must be acted out with the proper hand movements and facial expressions.] "I'm Joe Blow, I just finished making a speech at lunch in Cincinnati and I'm on my way to Mansfield to speak to the Chamber of Commerce. I'm going to talk to them about how to use psychology in sales and public relations. I'm also going to tell them how to bring industry into the town and get it booming again. They're going to give me three hundred dollars for it." And that fellow just looked at me and said, ". . . six, seven, eight, nine, ten."

Told properly, this story will shatter your audience. I know a man who has learned to tell it so well that people often come up afterwards to sympathize with him for his unnerving experience. Needless to say, when he tells it his audience roars—and he has them in his hip pocket from then on.

Here is another example:

I had a pleasant flight in from New York. I sat next to an old fellow who must have been about eighty years old. This was his first airplane ride. The stewardess spotted him right away and went out of her way to take good care of him. She gave him some orange juice and told him it would keep his stomach settled. She put a pillow behind his head to make him comfortable and she gave him some chewing gum and told him, "This will keep your ears from popping at high altitudes." When we were getting off the plane here in Chicago, the stewardess asked him if he enjoyed his flight. "Oh, I enjoyed it fine," he said, "but before I go, please tell me how to get this chewing gum out of my ears."

The number of stories that can be adapted as though they happened on the way to the meeting is endless; the oldest trick in vaudeville is still good for laughs. You can also begin those stories by saying "you overheard a lady say" or you "saw a little boy" or "the man sitting next to me said" or you were "reading the newspaper" and so on. Phrases like these will make your stories ring true.

Funny stories about your arrival at the hotel make good openers too, because everyone in the audience has had a similar experience. Here is a sample routine about arriving at a hotel.

I'm happy to be in Miami Beach. I've never been treated more warmly. What a beautiful hotel! I was given the red-carpet treatment and ushered to my room. While the bellman was turning on the lights and the television and showing me where the bathroom was, I said to him, "I thought this was supposed to be an ocean-view room." "It is, it is," he answered. "Just pull that dresser over by the window and stand on it and you can see a speck of blue water right over that way." [In a place where everyone wanted ocean-view rooms and couldn't get them, this line will always get a hearty chuckle.]

This is the first time I have ever been in one of these fancy Miami Beach hotels, and I wanted to be sure and tip the bellman properly, so I asked him about it. I said, "What is the average tip here in Miami Beach?" He said, "Five dollars." [You'll get a laugh here.] I didn't want to be cheap so I gave him the five dollars. But I said to him, "If five dollars is the average tip here, you must be getting rich." "No, sir. In all the time I've worked here, this is the first average I was ever able to get." [Although this is one of the oldest hotel jokes in the books, it will still make the audience laugh if you tell it well.]

This is one of the finest hotels I've ever stayed in. They think of everything for their guests. On the night table by my bed they placed a book for me to read. It was called *The Bedside Reader*. It had all sorts of things in it. Inside the front cover it said, "Suggested things to read before you go to sleep at night." [At this point hold up an imaginary book while you read the front inside cover.] It said, "If you're down in the dumps and discouraged, read page ------." I turned to that page and read it. It was interesting, and I looked at the front cover again. It said, "If you are lonesome and restless, read page ------." I turned to that page and read it. Then at the bottom I noticed that some very thoughtful person had written in pen and ink, "If you're still lonesome and restless, call Atlantic 896-8047 and ask for Irene."

You will notice that all of the preceding openers are about you, the speaker. You are the butt of the jokes. Audiences enjoy this kind of humor. They know that no matter what you are going to say in your speech, you are the kind of fellow who can "take it" as well as "dish it out."

Another category of laugh-getting openers that lends itself to good-natured teasing and lots of laughs comprises stories told on the celebrities present. In general, there is nothing wrong with joshing the man who introduced you or the president of the club or the program chairman or any other prominent member. However, the man should be well known and well liked or else your humor may misfire. If a man is the president of a club it is safe to asume that the audience knows him—and surely he wouldn't be president if they didn't like him.

First, show the audience that you can "take it" by telling

a story or two on yourself. Then you can slip in a story about someone at the head table who is in full view of the entire audience. The number of stories that can be used for this purpose would fill several books. Listed below are a few good examples.

Here is an opener that will never be forgotten by the members of a certain luncheon club. It illustrates how humor can be made relevant to the particular speaking occasion. The speaker arrived half an hour early and was chatting with the program chairman. In the course of conversation the chairman happened to mention that the president of the club was a funeral director. The speaker thought about it for a moment and remembered an old story he had carefully stored in his mental filing cabinet. He excused himself briefly and rushed into a men's furnishings store in the lobby of the hotel. He bought a bow tie, and replaced the four-in-hand tie he was wearing with his newly purchased bow. Now he was ready. After he was introduced, he started his speech:

I have never been treated more graciously or with warmer hospitality than I have received here. About half an hour ago, when I was still upstairs in my room, someone knocked on the door. It was your President Bill. He introduced himself and said he had come up to the room to escort me to the luncheon. I asked him to come in and wait a minute for me. I told him I'd be ready as soon as I could get my tie tied. I was having all kinds of trouble with it. When my wife travels with me I use one of those bow ties that needs to be tied because she can tie it for me. When I travel alone she packs one of those little snap-on bow ties. This time by accident she put in the wrong tie—the one someone else has to tie for me. I was having all kinds of trouble with it and President Bill said, "Maybe I can help you with it." And I said, "Yes, sir, please. Can you tie one of these things?" "Certainly," he said. "Just lie down on the floor."

This is a variation of the "it happened on the way to the meeting" story where the story is told on the program chairman:

I went by Mr. Chairman's office this morning and we walked over to the hotel together. Outside the hotel a panhandler stopped us. I bypassed him and pretended I didn't see him, but he buttonholed Mr. Chairman. He asked Mr. Chairman for a couple of bucks to get something to eat, and Mr. Chairman said, "No, I don't give money to tramps, especially to one as run-down and seedy-looking as you. But since it is cold and rainy and we're heading for a quick one in the bar before lunch, suppose I buy you a drink. That will warm you up, at least." "No, thank you, sir. I don't drink." "Well," Mr. Chairman said, "here's a cigar. Smoke it—it will make you feel better." "No, thank you," the bum said, "I don't smoke." I was wondering what Mr. Chairman was going to say to that, and he said, "Look, I don't give money to bums. It's against my principles. Since you are so persistent, though, I'll tell you what I'll do. Right after lunch I'm putting a couple of bucks on a horse that is running at Tropical Park. To show you I'm a good sport, I'll put two dollars on him for you. How's that?" "I appreciate your thoughtfulness, mister, but I don't gamble. All I want is some money for something to eat." That moved Mr. Chairman. He said, "Okay, you win. I'll buy you a steak dinner, but only on one condition. As soon as this dinner is over I want to drive you out to my house to meet my wife. I want her to take one look to see what happens to a man who doesn't drink, or smoke, or gamble."

Here is an especially good story to tell about the chairman when you are at a private company party.

A man went to see the doctor the other day with a stomachache. The doctor told him not to worry because a stomachache would be easy to cure. He took X rays and gave the man a blood test and a metabolism test. And the doctor said, "You just wait outside until the tests are completed and then we'll prescribe for you." That's what the man did and after a while the doctor called him in and said, "Well, you must feel pretty good right now." "No, I don't," the man said. "This gnawing pain in my stomach is about to kill me. It's been getting worse and worse. What makes you think I feel good?" "Because there's nothing the matter with you, that's why," the doctor said. "There's nothing organically wrong with you. I can't figure out what's causing the stomach pains unless it's some kind of occupational disease. Tell me, what sort of work do you do?" "I'm a truck driver. I work for Mr. Chairman." "You work for Mr. Chairman!" the doctor said. "Why in the world didn't you say so when you first came to see me? Here's a dollar. Go get something to eat."

When you are looking for a story to tell about the chairman or another prominent individual, his business or profession may provide some laughs. You will have to do a little research. Some examples of stories about different occupations are given below with hints on how to lead into them.

If Mr. Chairman is the owner of a furniture store:

I certainly want to thank Mr. Chairman for his gracious hospitality. I stopped by his beautiful furniture store this morning before coming to the luncheon. He showed me all through the place and told me some fascinating stories about his work. He told me that last year he won first prize for selling more furniture than any other store of the same size in the state. He won a ten-day all-expense-paid trip to Paris and he described his trip to me. He said the only thing that worried him was the fact that he couldn't speak a word of French. He told me about arriving in Paris and checking into his hotel late in the afternoon. At dinner time he decided he would get something to eat and perhaps do some sightseeing. When he got off the elevator and stepped into the lobby he noticed there was a pretty girl sitting on a couch. He walked over to her and said, "Do you speak English?" [There may have been a few snickers in the audience up to this point, but your next remark, an aside, will get a big laugh.] He was looking for a guide, you know! The young lady didn't say anything but she moved over and Mr. Chairman sat down beside her. He told me all about it. He said, "You don't need to know the language in that town." [Laugh] He said that the girl was a mind reader. [Laugh] She took out a pencil and paper and began to draw pictures for him. [You hold up your hand and write on it as though you were writing on a piece of paper.] She drew a picture of a wine glass. Mr. Chairman said he knew what that meant. All he had to do was to nod his head up and down and soon they were in a café drinking champagne. After the young lady had consumed a couple of bottles of champagne, she began to read his mind again. This time she drew a picture of a stage and put some dancing girls on it. [Repeat the motions of drawing.] All Mr. Chairman had to do was to nod his head and in a few minutes they ended up at a nightclub. After the show was over and they had returned to the hotel lobby, Mr. Chairman said she began to read his mind again. This time she drew a picture of a four-poster bed. And Mr. Chairman said, "How in the world she knew I was in the furniture business, I'll never know." [This story will get your speech off like a rocket from Cape Kennedy.]

If the chairman is the president of the local gas company:

The other afternoon a lady was doing her housework while her little boy was playing in the backyard. She happened to look out of the kitchen window in time to see him climb up on the fence and tear his brand-new dungarees. She went out, grabbed him and sent him back into the house as fast as he could go. "Get in there and change your clothes," she shouted. She stayed in the yard long enough to pick up his toys, and then she came back inside. As she walked into the kitchen, there in the middle of the floor were his dungarees where he had dropped them. She knew where he was because she could hear some noise coming from the utility room, so she called, "I know where you are. What are you doing in there, running around without any pants on?" And the voice that came back was the president of the gas company: "No, lady, I'm just reading your gas meter."

If the president of the club is a physician:

While we were eating lunch, Dr. President was telling me how long he had been practicing medicine. He told me about his first case. He had just opened his office when a man rushed through the door screaming and shouting, "Hurry, Doctor, hurry. Come help Harry. We were down at the barbershop practicing with the barbershop quartet and Harry was playing the mouth organ and somebody came in and slapped him on the back and he swallowed it. He's blue in the face. Hurry." Dr. President told me he was so surprised that he just stood there a minute without saying anything and finally the man shouted, "Well, Doc, what are you thinking?" And Dr. President said, "I was just thinking your friend sure was lucky that he wasn't playing a piccolo."

If you are introduced by a Baptist minister:

Not long ago the Baptist minister in our town had a terrible experience. He had been attending a special meeting of the finance committee. They had counted the proceeds from the all-day bazaar and had given the minister $480 to deposit in the bank in the morning. It was late at night and as the minister was walking home down a dark street, he was held up. The robber stuck a gun in the minister's stomach and said, "Give me your money." The minister gave him six dollars that he had in his wallet, and then the robber said, "What's in your other pocket?" "I'll not give you that," the minister said. "That's $480 of the church's money. I'm a Baptist minister, and you'll only get that money over my dead body." The robber said, "Oh, I'm sorry. I didn't know you were a Baptist preacher. I can't rob you. After all, I'm a Baptist myself."

If the program chairman is a veterinarian:

I certainly enjoyed chatting with Dr. Chairman during dinner. He was recounting some of his professional experiences to me. He told me about the man who suffered a broken leg when he was thrown from his horse in the woods last summer. He told me about the man's horse. When the horse realized his master couldn't move, he came alone to Dr. Chairman's house and banged on the back door and led Dr. Chairman to the man lying in the woods. Dr. Chairman said that was the smartest act he had ever seen a horse perform. Of course, I don't see anything so smart about it. A man lying in the woods with a broken leg and the stupid animal brings a horse doctor.

If the chairman is a lawyer:

It's always good to get acquainted with folks. Especially when you find you have mutual friends. I have a close friend who is a client of Mr. Chairman's. Last year my friend had trouble with a fellow who sold him some land that turned out to be under water. My friend was telling me about it. He said that he went to the fellow and demanded his money back. I asked him what luck he had and he said, "Why, I didn't have any luck with him. He told me to go to the devil." I asked him, "And then what did you do?" And he told me, "Why, when he wouldn't give me my money back and told me to go to the devil, I went straight to Mr. Chairman."

If there is a prominent guest who is running for political office:

When I found out that I was supposed to introduce the Honorable Mr. Candidate tonight, I was puzzled about how to address him. I thought I might call him the Honorable Mr. So-and-so, or I could call him my long-time friend Joe So-and-so, or I could even call him my old buddy Joe. I wasn't sure how he would like to be introduced, so I asked him. I said, "When I introduce you tonight, what would you like me to call you?" And he said, "If it's all right with you, just call me Senator."

A great opener for a banquet is the old letter-writing routine. For it to be effective, you should write your own material. To help you get the feel of it, here is a sample routine with suggestions for preparing and delivering the material.

After your introduction, you might begin your speech this way: "I'm a bit embarrassed after that gracious introduction. My problem is that I don't know how long I'm supposed to speak. I wrote to Mr. Chairman and asked him, but I never received a reply to my letter. Then, just a few minutes ago, as he was getting ready to introduce me, he leaned over and whispered, 'Don't forget what I said in my letter.' And that's why I'm embarrassed, because as I was driving out of my driveway this morning, my wife asked me if I had everything I needed and if I was prepared for my speech. I told her that I didn't know how long I was supposed to talk because I had never received an answer from Mr. Chairman. She said, 'Oh, I forgot to tell you. A letter came yesterday. And just to make sure you wouldn't overlook it, I put it in the inside pocket of your coat.' And I reached in my pocket and there it was. But I couldn't read it while I was driving and I guess I forgot all about it until Mr. Chairman reminded me of it now. It's a bit embarrassing for me. I know I am not supposed to read my mail in public, but I guess I should take a look at this letter before I begin my speech."

At this point you reach into your pocket and pull out an envelope. If you have told the story well up to this point, you will have a roomful of curious people, anxious to know what is in the letter. They will be watching you carefully. Everything you do and say must look and sound like the truth. Be sure the envelope and its contents look genuine. You can accomplish this effect by preparing the letter beforehand with painstaking care.

First, you must have an authentic envelope from Mr. Chairman—one that has been through the mails. When his letter inviting you to speak arrived at your office, you cut it open so carefully that the envelope looks as though it has not been touched. Next, you cut off the top of his letterhead and pasted it to the top of a clean piece of paper. This gave you a letterhead on which to write. (People can spot a plain sheet of paper with no printing at the top. In addition, many people in the audience have probably received letters from Mr. Chairman, and they might be able to recognize his letterhead if they see it in your hands. This part of the show must look authentic.)

After you have prepared the letterhead, you write your routine on it. Leave some room to insert the names of a few local individuals in the funny stories that you have in your repertoire. You can pick up pertinent information from the chairman while you are seated together at the head table having dinner.

Now all you have to do is read the letter. When you read it, read it in a halting manner, as someone might do who is reading something aloud that he has never seen before. Be careful of the laughs. When they come, allow enough time for the laughter to subside before you continue to read. Everyone in the audience should be able to hear every word.

You remove the envelope from your pocket. Tear it open. (Nobody should be able to see that it has been carefully slit at the end.)

"My, he wrote a long letter." Wave it for all to see. "All I asked him was how long I was supposed to speak. Well, here is what he says:

Dear Mr. Speaker. It really doesn't matter how long you speak, but I do have a few suggestions about what you should say. Please don't talk about politics. We've heard enough of that topic lately, and besides, I'm the only member of the club who knows anything about politics anyway. [Laugh] Remember our wives will be there that night, and you know how stupid women are about politics. [Laugh] How about working your speech this way: I'll give you a real fancy introduction. You write it out and I'll memorize it. Then you can come back by saying something nice about me. [Laugh] You might mention that I'm the biggest automobile dealer in town. [Laugh] Business hasn't been too good lately and a plug or two from you might help. [Laugh] After that you might say something about me personally—how hard I work [Laugh] or how smart I am—and, of course, mention how modest I am. [Laugh] My wife, Jane, will be there and I'd like her to hear somebody say something good about me, just one time. [Laugh]

Please try to be subtle. Don't let it seem as though you and I collaborated on this ahead of time or it might make some of the other members of the club jealous. For example, if you mention my business, George McGeorge would want you to say something nice about that awful telephone service of his. [Laugh] Another fellow who always tries to get free publicity is Billy Reed, the undertaker. He would want you to mention his grade one super deluxe lay-away plan. [Laugh] Also, you may get a letter from the president of the club with some suggestions about your speech. Ignore them. [Laugh] He may be the president, but I'm the man who runs things in the club. [Laugh] Good luck with your speech. Sincerely, Mr. Chairman.

Be careful not to laugh while you are reading the letter. Sometimes the audience laughs so hard that it is difficult for you to keep a straight face. Never drop the

norable way to ring down the curtain—that is, with
nor. If you want people to remember you and what
said, the old vaudeville rule "always leave them
hing" still holds true.

f course, there are many speeches that do not lend
nselves to humorous endings. The stirring speech by
Winston Churchill calling on the British to fight to
last ditch in World War II had to end on a note of
eful determination—not with a belly laugh. However,
are talking about the great majority of after-dinner,
after-luncheon and in-between speeches, which num-
over twenty thousand a day in the United States. In
st of these cases audiences would be happier if the
eches ended on a note of levity.

hilarious closing story can accomplish several ob-
ives for you. First, it ensures that the audience will
ember you, the speaker, perhaps even better than
at you said. Second, it lets the audience know that the
ech is over as crisply as it began. Third, it gives you an
ortunity to nail down at least one point in your
ech that your listeners can take away with them (this
 be the only point they will be able to remember).
est of all, the humorous closing gives you complete
trol of the timing of your dramatic exit from the po-
n. You are in full command. You tell your funny story,
 as the laughter rises from the audience you step
k, bow and allow the applause to blend with the
hter. You can't have a better combination than that.
here are two points to keep in mind when you want
ear laughter as well as hand claps. First, you must
e a story that will create uproarious laughter, the
y-laugh kind of story. After you have put together a
cine of surefire laugh-getters and have practiced them
he point of perfection, always close with one of your
 stories. If you have only two "barn-burners" and a

pretense that this is a genuine letter that you are reading
for the first time.

This is only an example. Don't copy it. Write your own.
The format is so flexible that you can do almost anything
you want with it.

Always remember that the purpose of your humorous
openers is to attract attention, to create a sense of expectancy, to build a warm rapport with your audience,
to relax them and, finally, to relax yourself.

Practice your openers. The skill of launching a speech
with laughter can be developed. Once you have perfected
the technique so that your speeches are greeted with
roars of laughter, you will discover that you are enjoying
your audience and they are enjoying you—and who could
ask for a better beginning?

69

V
HILARIOUS CLOSERS

Bringing the curtain down on a speech is not an easy matter. In fact, it's much harder to conclude a speech than it is to start one.

Your speech begins with a sharp break. The chairman says, "I now present . . ." and the next thing you know you are on your feet, facing the audience. You may not be ready. You may not have a good opening remark on the tip of your tongue. You may not even be happy about having to make the speech. But there you are—you have been introduced and your speech must start.

Up to that moment, you have had some help. The person who has introduced you has set the stage and raised the curtain for you.

The conclusion is not as simple. There isn't anybody

there to help you—no gracious and ea[sy]
man who will step up and say, "Th[ank you for the]
speech. Thank you." Closing a speech[is a different]
proposition. You are standing there a[lone and must]
deliver the concluding remarks witho[ut any as]
sistance.

The ending of a speech is not alwa[ys as]
well defined as the opening. Theref[ore some]
allow their closing words to become[... Some]
speakers stop too abruptly. They look a[round,]
apologize for the late hour, then mu[mble and]
sit down. Others begin to sputter and [...]
If the audience has been especially rec[eptive, speak]
ers are captivated by their own succe[ss and refuse]
to end their talks. I once asked a ma[n who talked]
for an hour and a half why he had t[... "An]
odd thing happened tonight," he said. [... I had]
timed for exactly thirty minutes, but [seeing how]
much the audience was enjoying it, I [... cheat]
them by stopping. I just had to go on. [... of]
me."

Probably the worst way to end a s[peech is to ask]
for questions from the floor. To begin[... if you know]
your subject and your audience, you [have cov]
ered every point that would be of inte[rest. Ques]
tions are then unnecessary. Furthermo[re, if you]
have ever suffered through a speech [followed by a]
question-and-answer period, you are a[ware that most of]
the questions had already been answer[ed in the speech]
and that many of them were asked mer[ely to let the ques]
tioner show off. Moreover, in nearly ev[ery such ques]
tion period makes the meeting run past[its closing]
time.

Although there are many effectiv[e ways to end a]
speech, we are going to concentrate [...]

half a dozen "chucklers," use one of your barn-burners for your opener, and the other for the closer.

Second, follow the same rules for telling a funny story that are described in Chapter II. That is, don't procrastinate with a note of apology in your voice or explain that you are going to end your speech with a funny story. It is a good idea to let your audience know you are coming to the end of your speech, so they will be ready to applaud, but when you begin your closing story, slide into it gracefully. Tell it. Take your bows. And sit down. Never utter another word after your last funny punch line.

Here are some stories that make good endings. Each paragraph below is a word-for-word closing routine that can be altered and modified to fit nearly any public-speaking engagement.

I hope my brief remarks today about water pollution haven't bored you. Not long ago I was invited to speak at the state mental hospital to a group who were receiving psychiatric treatment. I had been talking for about two minutes when a fellow in the back stood up and shouted, "You're no psychiatrist. You don't know what you are talking about. Besides, you're talking too much. Shut up and sit down." (Act the story out. Point to the back.) I stopped and said to the superintendent, I'll wait a minute until you put him out. "Put him out?" the superintendent said. "Certainly not. That poor fellow has been here eight years, and that's that first time he has ever said anything that makes sense." And the more you think about it, maybe that fellow did make sense—and that's what I'm going to do. Then do it. Smile and sit down.

When you do not have a dramatic and resounding conclusion to your remarks, this story will bring your speech to a sharp conclusion.

As I close my talk today I just want to say that I hope I don't have the same sort of experience I did when I spoke recently in Bucks County, Pennsylvania. That's where the Amish live. They have the Amish, the Dunkards and the Mennonites. [Itemize them on your fingers.] After my speech I had to take a bus back to the hotel in town and I sat in the back across from a Dunkard preacher. He had on his long black coat and that odd-looking black hat they wear. He had a beard down to about here. [Show how far down it came.] At the next corner, when the bus stopped, a drunk got on. He was really tipsy. He got into a fight with the bus driver. They had quite an argument over the fare and after a while the bus driver quieted the drunk and sent him to the rear of the bus. He staggered back to where we were and as he was holding on to the strap [hold on to the strap and wobble like a drunk] he looked down at that preacher. "Well, look at you. All dressed up in that funny-looking uniform. And wearing a beard. What are you anyway, a wrestler? What's going on around here, a carnival or something?" The preacher jumped up and stood there in all of his dignity and said, "I'll have you know I'm a Dunkard pastor." "Well, shake hands, friend" [hold out your hand like the drunk did], the drunk said, "that's what the bus driver just called me."

Then step away from the lectern. Don't come back for another single word, not even "Thank you." Your speech is over.

This closing is appropriate for any type of anniversary celebration:

"I want to say again how happy I am to have been invited to speak on the occasion of your fortieth anniversary. This has been a very gay affair. I think this is the way it should be. It reminded me of the farmer's wife. She woke him up one morning and said (shake him) 'Wake up, today's our fortieth wedding anniversary. I think we ought to celebrate. What do you say we kill a chicken?' Her husband rolled over and said, 'Why in the world do you want to punish a poor chicken for something that happened forty years ago?' "

And here we come to a point of judgment. If you have concluded your speech ahead of schedule and have a few minutes of your allotted time left, and if that story stimulated a big laugh, you might want to give your audience a bit more for their money. Here is a good follow-up story. "The wife of a friend who plays golf with me now and then was complaining about the amount of time my friend spent playing golf. 'You don't love me anymore,' she said. 'All you do is think about golf. Why, you don't even remember the date of our anniversary.' 'I certainly do,' my friend said. 'It was the day after I shot an eagle on the fourth hole at Westview Country Club.' "

Here is a rather soft and gentle ending rather than a great belly whopper. "At this point, I wonder if I'm not like the country boy who was walking through the woods with his girl friend one Sunday afternoon. He put his arm around her and looked into her pretty blue eyes and said, 'Honey, I love you more than anything in the world. Will you marry me?' And she didn't hesitate a second. 'Oh, yes, I'll marry you.' They continued to walk through the woods and neither one of them said anything. After an hour of complete silence, the young lady turned to her boyfriend and said, 'Honey, why don't you say something?' He looked again into her pretty blue eyes and said, 'It seems to me that I've probably said too much as it is.' "

If your speech has been filled with dire predictions or if it has dealt with a variety of local problems, such as water and air pollution, or the shortage of schoolrooms, or other community problems, this story makes a fitting ending. "From some of the things I have talked about today, you may think we have a lot of troubles facing us. I thought of the troubles of a friend of mine. The other morning, before he could get out of his house and head for work, he had four long-distance calls. Everyone seemed to have a problem. And everybody wanted him to get on a plane that very day and come help out. He finally told his wife to forget about his breakfast. He rushed out of the house as fast as he could. Then, when he stepped into the garage he discovered his car wouldn't start. So he called a taxi to take him to work. While he was waiting for the taxi, his boss in Chicago called him about another urgent problem. Finally, the taxi came and my friend rushed out, piled into the back seat, and yelled, 'All right, let's get going.' The taxi driver turned around and said, 'Where do you want me to take you?' 'I don't care where I go,' he shouted. 'I've got problems everywhere.' "

When your speech has included a number of different subjects, this story will bring down the house:

I guess I have covered everything today, except maybe the weather. So before I sit down I might as well talk about that for a moment. Last winter in Clark County we had some real cold weather. Four inches of snow. Of course, when we have a blizzard like that we shut down the schools. So we closed the schools for three days. Then, on the first day that school was open, a teacher noticed a little fellow in the front row with his head on his desk. He was sound asleep. She woke him up [shake the kid slightly] and said, "What's the matter? You're not sick, are you? Why are you asleep?" And the little fellow said, "No, I'm not sick. It was the chicken thieves last night. You know, they've been stealing our chickens and Pa said the next time they came around he was going to get himself a couple of dead chicken thieves. And last night in the middle of the night he heard 'em. You never heard so much noise in the chicken house. Pa jumped up out of bed and ran to put on his trousers. He ran out in his nightshirt. He grabbed his shotgun by the back door and loaded both barrels [point to the back door and grab that gun] and he put his fingers on both triggers, and he tiptoed out through all that snow to the chicken house. He heard 'em inside and he was easing that door open real easy like. [Bend down and sight the shotgun you are holding in your hand. You're sneaking up on a chicken house full of chicken thieves.] And you know that old dog of ours named Rover? He came up behind Pa with his cold nose. [Try a count of five and look at the teacher absolutely wide-eyed.] And we was up all night long last night at our house, cleaning and pickin' chickens."

This story would fit any speech—long or short. "I think I have said enough today. I think I'd better sit down before I get hoarse. That's always embarrassing for a speaker. Three weeks ago I had laryngitis. It began rather mildly at the office in the morning, but by the time I was ready to go home I could hardly whisper. I thought it might be a good idea to stop by a doctor's office. A friend told me about a good ear, nose and throat specialist who lived right on my way home. So I stopped at his house and rang the doorbell. In about half a minute the door was opened by the doctor's wife. She sure was a beauty, I'll say that for her. And I said (whisper this; remember, you have laryngitis) 'Is the doctor home?' and she said (whisper) 'No. He's out of town. Come on in.'"

There are times when you may have been trying to

sway an audience to your point of view but from their reaction you feel that you haven't convinced many of them. Here is an ending that will make you the hero of the day even though everyone may not have agreed with what you said:

I want to thank you for listening to me so attentively. I hope I have been able to convince a few of you. On the other hand, I may be like a preacher we had in our town when I was a boy. He was the minister of the Christian church and preached there every Sunday. Then one time a group in the next town started a church. Everybody in that town went in on it and they built a community church. [Hold your hands up to indicate a church.] Our minister used to go out there and preach every Sunday afternoon for them—free. He'd been preaching for a few weeks when a group in the congregation started a campaign to get a name for their new church. They didn't want it to be called a community building. The minister thought that was a good idea, especially if they called it a Christian church. After the usual committee work, the congregation was ready to vote on the question one Sunday afternoon. The minister said, "Today we're going to vote on whether or not to call this a Christian church. Before we vote I wonder if anyone has anything to say on the subject." I'll never forget it. An old fellow stood up in the back [point to him] and said, "Yes, I've got something to say. I know it won't do any good because it looks like this meeting is rigged. But I have been a Baptist for forty years and you're not going to make a Christian out of me."

Regardless of your subject, you might sum up and close with this story:

Before I sit down I want to say again in simple language, "We need better schools and better schools take money." I may have used several thousand words to explain my position, but I always have to come back to that simple statement: "We need better schools and better schools take money." I learned to pound home my point like this when I was a boy. When I was in the eighth grade we had an oratorical contest. I didn't win it. A fellow in school named George Sanderson won. We always felt it was unfair because he had memorized Patrick Henry's famous give-me-liberty-or-give-me-death speech. He won the school contest and then went on to win the county contest, and finally he won the state contest. He won so many prizes that it went to his head. He developed a Patrick Henry complex. No matter what you said to him he would twist the answer around to make it end with his pet phrase, "Give me liberty or give me death." We got so tired of hearing it that several of us went to complain to the teacher about George. She said we shouldn't worry. She had noticed it too and felt that it was time to bring him back to normal. She said the way to do it would be to get George in front of the class and ask him a question that he couldn't answer, much less twist around. And that is what she did. One day after recess she called him to the front of the class and said to him [you are now the teacher looking down at a boy], "George, I'm going to ask you a question and I want a short, concise answer. Here is the question: What is the colic? Give me a definition of colic." George looked up at her [Look up at the teacher], scratched his head for a minute and said, "I'm not a doctor or a scientist, but according to my understanding, the colic is an over-accumulation of atmosphere confined within the framework of the human anatomy crying, 'Give me liberty or give me death.'"

The next story not only makes an uproarious ending, but it will help you clinch the main point of your speech.

Before I sit down, I want to emphasize what I have been saying about recreation for young people by reminding you that when you are betting on youth today, you are betting on a sure thing. Nothing is as rewarding as betting on a sure thing. Down in Danville, Kentucky, one time at the county fair, they were having a horse race. When the window opened to take bets that morning, the first man there was a farmer and he said, "I want to put five hundred dollars on Blue Belle, to win." He took the tickets, and put them in his pocket and headed down behind the barns. [Put the tickets in your pocket.] About half an hour later he came back again. He had been drinking a little Kentucky mountain dew. He wasn't drunk, but he had gained a lot of enthusiasm for that horse. He walked up to the window and said, "Give me another five hundred dollars' worth of tickets on Blue Belle to win. That's the fastest race horse that ever ran on any track in Kentucky. He is sure to win." [Tell this with the man's enthusiasm.] He put those tickets with his others and went back to the bottle down behind the barn. Finally, when the bugle blew for post time, back he came again. By this time he had finished the bottle and he was staggering a bit. [Stagger a bit.] He was also talking to himself. As he approached the ticket window there was a line in front of it, and he had to wait his turn. He was standing there talking to himself: "A thousand dollars on old Blue Belle. The mortgage on the farm on Blue Belle." A man standing in front of him turned and said, "My friend, I can't help but hear what you are saying. I'd like to give you a little advice. You should step out of line and save yourself a thousand dollars. There are six horses in that race and Blue Belle is not the fastest horse. I happen to know because I own Blue Belle." The old farmer looked at him for a moment and then said, "Well, all I can say, old buddy, is that it sure is going to be a mighty slow race, isn't it? Because I own the other five."

Here are stories that can make your point as you step back from the lectern to the tune of laughter and applause. "Today I have tried to give you a quick look at some of the tenets of public relations and show how they can be applied to our industry. Many of our problems can be solved by a careful study and a diligent application of the principles of good business. There are no magic words. The nearest thing to magic words are those we use to try to convince traffic cops. A painter who was working over at the bank had parked his truck in a ten-minute parking zone, and he fastened a note to the windshield with these magic words: 'Painter working inside.' Later, when the painter went out to his truck, he found a ticket under the windshield wiper with these words written across it: 'Policeman working outside.'"

"As I leave here today, I hope you won't get the idea that I am a warmonger. I want peace, but I don't want it the way the old circus performer arranged things. Two circus buddies who hadn't seen each other in a long time met and were chatting. 'How's it going?' the first asked. 'It couldn't be any better,' the other said. 'I have a new act. With the world so interested in peace, I figured out an act where I have a lion and a lamb performing together in the same cage.' 'That sounds like a good act,' his friend said, 'but you would think that they wouldn't get along too well together. Don't you ever have any trouble?' 'Yes,' said the other fellow. 'Now and then things don't go so well, but it really doesn't create too much of an inconvenience. All we have to do is buy another lamb.'"

You can often tie in your closing story with the season of the year. During the basketball season, this is a good way to end a speech. "I thank you for your attention. I have tried to present the story of our industry in a creditable manner. I hope I did better than the basketball player who was the star of the team at a small Catholic school in Massachusetts. The score was tied. The tension was high. Then the visitors fouled the star of the home team. He was given two free throws. He stepped up to the line with great confidence, crossed himself as he usually did, threw for the basket and missed. He repeated the performance. He crossed himself, threw and missed. A few minutes later, he was fouled again and was given two more free throws. He repeated the same procedure. He missed both times. Then he was fouled a third time. As he stepped up to the line and crossed himself before shooting, the priest who was sitting in the second row leaned over and whispered to the coach, 'Hurry and take that boy out of there. He's giving the church a bad name.'"

When your time is limited and you can only speak to the point, try this story for a closer. "Talking to you these past few minutes has been most delightful. I tried to stick to the subject that I came to talk about. When I was at the university we had an absent-minded professor. One evening he dropped in on his old friend, a doctor. They had a pleasant visit together and before they realized it a couple of hours had slipped by. As the professor was putting on his coat to leave, the doctor said, 'The family's all well, I suppose.' 'Good heavens,' the professor said. 'That reminds me why I came to see you. My wife's having a fit.'"

82

If you are no orator and know it, but have presented your proposition as best you could, this closing will endear you to the audience. "It has been a pleasure to speak to you today and I want you to know that I have been speaking to you directly from my heart. I wasn't trying to imitate anyone else. I learned better than that when I was in college. We had a big amateur night in connection with a school dance and I was on the program to do some impersonations. I had all the usual ones —Bogart, Cagney and the rest. When we got to the dance, we discovered that a rather famous singer had come along with the band. (I wouldn't dare mention his name.) I had his impersonation in my repertoire and I had really worked on it. When the show was over I was introduced to him. I was anxious to get a pat on the back from him and so I asked him, 'What did you think of my impersonation of you?' He looked at me and said, 'Well, all I can say is one of us is pretty lousy.' "

If you are working for a community cause, you may often find yourself talking to the same groups on the same subject year after year. When you find yourself in this situation, here is a closer that will get you a big hand. "I am grateful for the privilege of being invited here today to talk about the United Fund. I know you have heard the story many times, and I appreciate your listening to me again this year. When I was a boy in New England I worked after school in my uncle's clothing store. I'll never forget the day a new salesman for the local newspaper was trying to convince him to take an advertisement. 'I don't need to advertise,' my uncle said. 'I've been in business in this town for thirty years.' 'Tell me something,' the salesman said. 'I've just moved to town. What's that big, old-fashioned building up on the hill?' " (Point to the hill.) " 'That's the church,' my uncle said. 'How long has it been here?' the salesman wanted to know. 'About a hundred and fifty years,' my uncle said. 'Well, they still ring the bell every Sunday, don't they?' "

Your speech may have dealt with a lot of complicated subjects. These two stories would make humorous endings. "I have tried to explain some complex matters today. But maybe I'm like the local nurse back home who had been conducting a class for prospective fathers. She felt that somehow or other she had not reached us as she should. As she wound up her final lesson, she said, 'For five weeks I have been trying to teach you how to help your wives care for the new baby that is coming to live with you. If you forget everything else I have tried to teach you, remember this: When it's your turn to look after the baby, keep one end full and the other end dry, and you'll be all right.' "

"I hope I haven't confused you with anything I have said today. There was a young fellow who went shopping for his wife. He stood in the department store with a perplexed look on his face. Finally a clerk walked up to him and asked if he could be of help. 'Yes, you can,' the confused fellow said. 'I was supposed to buy either a camisole or a casserole, but I can't remember which.' 'I'm sure I can help you,' the clerk said, 'if you tell me what sort of chicken you want to put in it.' "

If you think you may run over your allotted time, have this story ready. "I hope my being here is not like an old friend of mine who lives in St. Petersburg. He's eighty-two years old and he always has dreamed of living to be a hundred. Last summer he went for his annual checkup and the doctor told him that he would have to give up drinking and smoking. 'And then will I live to be a hundred?' my friend asked. 'No,' the doctor said, 'but it will seem like it.' "

Here is a closer that will get a big laugh when you are speaking at the local country club and everyone is dressed in his evening clothes. "It was a pleasure to speak to you tonight and to be in such fine company. I feel like the drunk who was staggering down the street late at night on his way home. His minister happened to pass in his car, and he stopped and picked up the drunk and drove him home. When they arrived in front of the drunk's house the drunk said to the minister, 'Thanks for the ride home. Now just come up to the front door with me. I want my wife to see who I was out with tonight.' "

After a short luncheon talk, any one of these stories will get laughter and applause. "I thank you for inviting me to be a part of your luncheon meeting today. I want to thank you, too, for laughing at my efforts to tell a story or two. My wife thinks my stories are rather farfetched. I asked her the other day what she meant by farfetched. And she told me. 'Most of them were brought to this country on the *Mayflower*.' "

"Please let me thank you again for inviting me to share this delightful luncheon with you. I enjoyed speaking to you. You will also notice that I enjoyed my lunch. I'm not like the preacher who visited our church back home when I was a boy. We had an all-day-preaching-with-lunch-on-the-ground affair, and the minister was the first speaker after lunch in the afternoon. My aunt started to fill up a plate for him, but he said, 'No, thank you. I never eat before I preach. I find that if I do, I never preach a good sermon.' After his sermon was over, I heard my aunt say to my mother, 'As far as I am concerned, he might as well of et.' "

"Thank you for letting me speak to you today. I hope it was as good as a speech I made last week. Because after that one, when I had finished and sat down, everybody said it was the best thing I had ever done."

This story is a good way to end a company meeting where you have presented some new programs or ideas.

"I want to emphasize again that we have a new and exciting plan. And as you go back to your jobs today I want you to remember the two girls who were chatting during their coffee break. 'No girl should be discouraged,' said the first one. 'In this world there's a man for every girl, and a girl for every man. You can't improve on a plan like that.' 'I don't want to improve on it,' the second girl said, 'I just want to get in on it.'"

When you have spoken on behalf of a department or a group rather than as an individual, this closer will bring the curtain down with smiles. "On behalf of the Agriculture Department I want to thank you for inviting me here today. When Mr. Chairman called the director of the Department and asked for a speaker for your meeting, the director called me into his office and said to me, 'The Farm Bureau wants someone from the Department to attend their convention and speak to them very badly— and you're just the man who can do it.'"

This ending is perfect for anyone speaking on behalf of a government agency. "I have been happy to speak to you on behalf of the Post Office Department. I'm glad that most of you are married men. I think every man should marry, because there are just some things in the world that can't be blamed on the government."

This story suits a speech in which you have presented a controversial point of view. "Thank you for the opportunity to state my case here today. I have tried to convince you of the necessity of taking action. I wish I were as sure of results as the mother who was talking to her daughter about her forthcoming marriage. 'I'm so worried about marrying John,' the daughter said. 'He is an atheist and he doesn't believe there is a hell.' 'That's all right,' her mother said. 'Go ahead and marry him, and between the two of us I am sure we can convince him.'"

Now and then a speaker is asked to answer questions.

If you realize that the meeting is going to run overtime, and you want to end the question-and-answer period, here is a time-tested story that fits the situation. "I would like to stand here all day answering questions and talking about my favorite subject. But I think I should take the same advice that the mother cabbage gave to her off-spring. Once there was a little baby cabbage who said to his mother, 'Mommy, I'm worried about something. As I sit in this row of cabbages and grow and grow and grow day after day, how will I know when to stop grow-ing?' 'The rule to follow,' the mama cabbage said, 'is to quit when you are a head.'"

If you tell this story properly, it will get a big laugh. At the same time you can make your point clear:

The problems that we have talked about today have many ramifications. I hope I have been able to shed a little light on some of them. I only wish I could have explained all of them as well as a friend of mine ex-plained a problem to a friend of his. A bachelor said he would be glad to baby-sit with his sister's baby boy. About two hours after everyone had left for the theater, he was faced with a crisis. He was frantic, and he called a young father whom he knew and told him his troubles. The young father said, "Don't worry about it. Just follow these directions. [Use a napkin from the banquet table to act this one out.] Place the diaper in the position of a baseball diamond with you standing at bat. Next, fold second base to touch home plate. [Fold it.] Then, place the baby on the pitcher's mound with his head pointing toward center field. [Place the baby.] Then fold third base, first base, and home plate so they meet. [Fold.] Fasten in that position with a safety pin." [Pin it. Now look pleased with yourself.]

If you have had the crowd with you during your speech, this is a good way to end it. "When I was getting ready to come here tonight, my wife said to me, 'Remember to be a good sport.' She was reminding me about the sailor who was chatting with a young lady he had just met at a Red Cross canteen. 'What kind of sports do you like?' the sailor wanted to know. And the young lady told him, 'The kind that are free and easy with their money and know when to say good night and go home.'"

If your speech has been over thirty minutes long, and if it has been on a highly technical subject, you will absolutely bring down the house if you learn to tell this story properly:

I appreciate your patience in putting up with my talk today. I wasn't sure you would be able to stand me for this long. Like a widow in a small Southern town who decided to go into business for herself. She set up a bootleg operation in her home. It was down a dirt street, and the kids who used to play out front would watch the men come up on the porch and knock on the door. The conversation went something like this: "What do you want?" the woman asked. "You know what we want," the men would say, "we want some of that stuff." "You got any money?" the woman would say. "Yes," they would say, "we got two dollars." She would let them come into the living room and then she would sell them a jug of moonshine whiskey for two dollars. Then they would go down the street whistling and singing and looking real happy. One day, a couple of the kids out front decided to see what it was all about. So they knocked on the door and the conversation went something like this: "What do you want?" the woman asked. "You know what we want," a little fellow said, "we want some of that stuff." "You got any money?" she asked. "Yes 'um," the little boy said, "we got ten cents." "She figured she would teach them a lesson, so she asked them into the living room, took their dime away from them, banged their heads together, and then pitched them out into the street. The first little boy got up and dusted himself off and cried, "Dog-gone it, I don't think I could of stood two dollars' worth of that stuff."

Political stories told by politicians are especially welcomed by audiences. The best laugh getters are stories that the speaker tells on himself. They also make good closers.

I must close now, not because my speech is finished, but because I've got to get out on the street and begin to hustle up some more votes. [Laugh] The other day when I was out soliciting votes I ran into an old friend. I asked him to vote for me and he said he was sorry, but he couldn't vote for me. He told me he was a Republican—a born Republican. I asked him what he meant by a born Republican. "Well," he said, "my dad was a Republican, and my grandfather was a Republican, and I'm a Republican. I always vote the straight Republican ticket." I said to him, "That's no reason to vote for anybody. Do you mean to tell me that if your dad had been an idiot and your grandfather had been an idiot, that you'd be an idiot?" "No," my friend said, "I'd be just like you. I'd be a Democrat."

Here is a great closer for any kind of political rally. Adjust it to fit your speech and the meeting will end on a note of levity:

Be sure to vote tomorrow. And vote your convictions. Last election day a farmer was driving to town. He picked up two farmhands on the road and asked them where they were going. "We're going to town to vote," the first one said. "That's fine," the farmer said. "That's where I'm going. How are you going to vote?" "I'm a Democrat," the farmhand said. "I'm going to vote for the party." The farmer stopped his car and put the man out. As he drove down the road, he said to the other man, who was still in the car, "How are you going to vote?" It was fourteen miles to town and that man didn't want to walk, so he thought about it a minute and then said, "I'm gonna vote Republican." That must have pleased the farmer, because he didn't say anything. But as they passed a watermelon patch the farmer said, "Hey, there isn't anybody looking. How about climbing over the fence and picking a couple of melons? We'll eat them on the way to town." The farmhand did just that. As they were resting in the shade of a tree, eating the melons, the farmhand started laughing. "What's so funny?" asked the farmer. The farmhand said, "Here I've been a Republican for only twenty minutes and I'm stealing already."

This political story can be twisted into a thousand shapes. It is an old standby for bringing a speech to an uproarious end. "As the mayor of the city I am happy to welcome you and your fine organization. The other day I was visiting in Atlanta and ran into an old friend who had just heard that I had been elected mayor. He was trying to butter me up and he said, 'Congratulations on being elected mayor. I suppose you won because the people in your town know that you are honest and upright and always deal fairly with your customers.' And I had to tell him the truth. The real reason I was elected was because I was the only one running for the office."

When you have taken your campaign to a service club luncheon, you will leave the audience with a pleasant memory if you conclude with this story. "I hope that I have won some support here today. A young fellow studying political science asked his father, 'Dad, what is a traitor in politics?' 'Any man who leaves our party,' the boy's father said, 'and goes over to the other side is a traitor.' 'Well, what about a man who leaves his party and comes over to yours?' the boy asked. 'In that case,' the boy's father said, 'he'd be a convert, son, a real convert.'"

This one will get a laugh after you have been speaking against the Communist way of life. "It has been good talking to you today about the United States and Russia. All that I told you does not bring the difference between capitalism and communism into such sharp focus as the Russian who was shown a copy of a Sears, Roebuck catalog by an American tourist. 'Do you mean to tell me,' he said, 'that in America all of these things are available to the masses?' 'Available?' the American said. 'In America we have to beg people to buy them.'"

We come now to one of the greatest laugh-getting closers. The story is so versatile that it can be twisted to fit nearly any group that has invited you to speak—Lions or Kiwanians, Masons or Knights of Columbus, Methodists or Baptists:

It has been a great pleasure for me to speak to this fine Lions Club today. I certainly admire the work you men do in the community. Back in my home town I am a member of the Kiwanis Club. And we have a few projects that we are proud of. Before I sit down I'd like to tell you about our favorite project. Every year a committee from our Kiwanis Club picks up all the mail at the post office that has been addressed to Santa Claus. Then they take it over to our office and open it, and the committee makes sure that each child who has written to Santa Claus receives a gift. Three years ago, when the committee was opening the mail, they came across one letter that read: "Dear Santa

Claus, I hate to bother you with my problems, but my wife is in the hospital and I have just lost my job. We have eight children and unless you help us, we won't have a very good Christmas. I wonder if you would be a good Santa Claus and send me a check for six hundred dollars. Joe Henderson." "Why, I know him," one of the committee members said. "He's a member of the Lions Club. Anyway, throw it away, because we are supposed to help only children." "That may be so," said another member, "but here is a man who needs help. He must be pretty desperate or he wouldn't have written to Santa Claus. We ought to do something for him." After much discussion, the committee members decided to send him a gift out of their own pockets. Among themselves they made up a purse of three hundred dollars and sent it to him. They never received a reply from the man. Not a word of thanks. Not even an acknowledgment that he had received the money. Then, the following year, when the committee was opening Christmas mail, they ran across this letter: "Dear Santa Claus, I hate to bother you again with my problems. But my wife is back in the hospital again. I still don't have a job and all the kids are hungry. If you won't help us, we won't have a very good Christmas. I wonder if you would be a good Santa Claus and send me a check for six hundred dollars. Joe Henderson. P.S. Santa Claus, this year when you send me the money, please send it through the Lions Club. Last year you sent it through the Kiwanis Club and those dirty crooks kept half of it."

Like the openers in Chapter IV, these are only samples. Select your funny stories, develop half a dozen good closers, practice them, and you will "always leave them laughing."

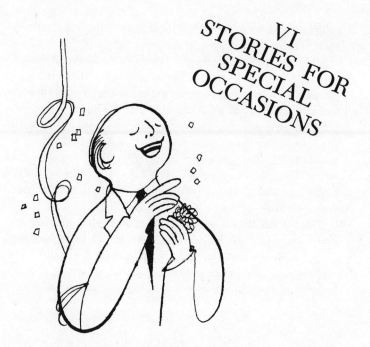

VI
STORIES FOR SPECIAL OCCASIONS

Up to this point we have discussed humor in general and have described the techniques and tricks for getting the most mileage out of a humorous story. We have given examples of a great many openers and closers and have explained the ways to make a story fit your particular needs.

In this chapter we'll take you one step further and show you how to prepare an entire humorous routine for a special occasion.

Good speakers are in great demand. Once you have learned to tell stories well, you will be invited to speak before a wide variety of audiences. Your popularity will increase and so will your reputation if you include several minutes of humor that harmonizes with the particular group or the purpose of its meeting.

Suppose, for example, that you have been invited to speak at a sales meeting. Here is an efficient method to follow in preparing your speech. First, put together the serious portions of your speech. Then look through several humor reference books for stories about salesmen in general. After that, select special stories that illustrate the main points of your message. Next, write out a smooth, flowing routine that will be easy for the audience to follow and that may even win your listeners to your way of thinking.

The following pages contain several routines for special occasions. We have used sales meetings to illustrate the technique, but we have also included routines that are appropriate to other groups. These are only samples, however; it is always best to prepare your own material.

FOR A SALES MEETING

When you are talking to salesmen, use a funny story or two to dramatize your points. For example, if you want to stress the value of using *ingenuity* in presenting a sales talk, tell them:

My secretary went into a department store the other day and was looking over some of the newest items at the perfume counter. She was hesitating over a small bottle when the salesgirl gave her the word. "I would advise you not to use that if you're bluffing." She bought it.

But talking about ingenuity in a sales talk, the other day I was getting a haircut and a shave, and I casually asked the barber what happened to Antonio, who used to work at the next chair. "Oh," the barber said, "that sure was a sad case. Antonio used to get despondent when business was slow. The other day when a customer refused to have a massage, Antonio went out of his head and cut the customer's throat with a razor. They had to send Antonio to the state mental hospital. By the way, you would like a massage, wouldn't you?"

That's ingenuity and so is this case. A man in a music store made up his mind that he was going to sell his lady customer something. "No," she said, "I don't want to buy a whistle for my little boy. The other day he almost swallowed one and I'm afraid he might choke to death." "Well," said the salesman, "how about buying him a nice bass fiddle."

Salesmen like to hear *success* stories. While you are relating actual case histories, throw in a few funny ones:

A friend of mine who owned a men's store put on a big sale in order to move some merchandise that had been in stock for several years. One of the suits was hideous. It was yellow with a blue stripe running down it. On the opening day of the sale, my friend hung that suit on the front rack and told his head clerk that he wanted the suit sold—or else. After lunch, when my friend came back to the store, he saw that the suit was gone. He went to congratulate his clerk and found him standing in the back room in absolute tatters. He was all bloody as though he had been in an accident. "I see you sold the suit," my friend said to him, "but don't tell me the customer did that to you." "Oh, no, sir," the clerk said. "The customer was perfectly satisfied, but his seeing-eye dog nearly tore me to pieces."

Talking about successful selling, my niece was going steady with a boy who was an atheist. This upset her father. He said, "We don't want you marrying an atheist. Why don't you talk religion to him? If he loves you, he'll listen. It's all a matter of doing the right kind of selling job." About two weeks later at breakfast, my niece seemed absolutely heartbroken. "What's the matter?" her father asked. "I thought you were making good progress talking religion to your boyfriend. Didn't it work?" "That's the trouble," she said. "It worked too well. I oversold him. Last night he told me he has decided to study to be a priest."

Persistence is also important in selling. Underscore the value of persistence with this routine.

The other night on television a reporter was interviewing a man who was celebrating his hundredth birthday. He said to the old man, "Tell me, to what do you attribute your longevity?" The old man had a quick answer. He said, "I never smoked, drank whiskey or stayed out late at night. And I always walked two miles every day." The reporter said, "I had an uncle who did that, but he didn't live to be a hundred. He died when he was seventy-two. How would you account for that?" And the old man said, "All I can say is he just didn't keep it up long enough."

Have you ever noticed how persistent kids can be? My sister's nine-year-old boy came to the table the other night without washing his hands and face. His mother said to him, "Go wash up. Night after night I have to tell you. Why don't you ever come to the table without my having to remind you about washing up?" "Well," he said, "it's always worth a try. Who knows? You might forget just once."

It would be great to have a sales force where everyone has as much persistence and stick-to-itiveness as the little girl who lives next door to me. She came home the other day and told her mother, "I certainly don't know what was bothering Mary all afternoon. She was mean and sassy and kept fussing and fighting."

STORIES FOR SPECIAL OCCASIONS

"In that case," her mother said, "I think you should have come on home." "Well," the little girl said, "I didn't. I just slapped her face and stayed."

Persistence is the quality that makes a man try and try again. A persistent salesman will keep at the job long after another man has given up and quit. There was a tramp in England who went to the back door of the famous pub George and the Dragon and asked for a handout. A woman answered the door and shouted at him, "Go on. Get out. We don't feed tramps here." Half an hour later he came back. The same woman answered the door and said, "Oh, it's you again. What do you want this time?" And the tramp said, "I wonder if I might have a few words with George."

When you want to illustrate the old saying "nothing succeeds like success," have a few *success* stories to tell.

A new vacuum cleaner salesman who was determined to succeed came to work one morning looking rather down in the mouth. "Cheer up," the sales manager said. "Things will work out. It's not easy at first but just practice your sales talk and call on enough people and you'll do all right." "Oh," the salesman said, "that's just the trouble. I went home last night and practiced my sales talk on my wife and now I have to buy her a vacuum cleaner."

I remember one year when I was on the board of directors of our local Chamber of Commerce, we were holding a testimonial dinner for the richest and most successful man in town. When the toastmaster presented the beautifully engraved plaque to our honored guest, he said, "Friends, when this man walked into our town forty years ago, it was nothing but a few shacks scattered along a dirt road. And the only earthly possessions he had were the clothes on his back, the shoes on his feet and a few things wrapped in a hand-kerchief slung over his shoulder. Today look how he has prospered. He owns his own business with branches all over the country. He owns apartment houses and office buildings. He is head of the bank and is a director of half a dozen companies. He has been the man most responsible for the progress of our fair city." After dinner an old friend went up to the great man and said, "I've known you for years and I've heard that story about you coming to town with all your possessions tied up in a handkerchief. I've often wondered what you had in that package." "Well," the great man said, "as far as I can remember back over forty years, it was a toothbrush, a razor and $500,000 in negotiable bonds."

I remember the first sales manager I ever worked for. He had a sign over his desk that read: "Secret of Success. Sell your wristwatch and buy an alarm clock." Another sales manager used to tell me, "Keep your eye on the ball, your shoulder to the wheel, and your ear to the ground." I tried it, but I couldn't ever get any work done in that position. He is the same sales manager who announced a big sales contest one time. He gave everybody goals and quotas and made a stir-ring sales talk to all of us. He didn't tell us what the prize was, so I asked him. I said, "What does the win-ner get?" And he said, "The winner gets to keep his job."

Everybody has his own ideas about success. When I used to travel in the mountains of Kentucky, I ran into an old farmer who told me how successful he had been. "Why," he told me, "when I came to Kentucky from Tennessee thirty years ago, I didn't have a dime to my name. Today I have thirteen kids and eleven dogs."

When I was a boy we had a smart aleck in school with us. He moved to Chicago and found that he was well-suited to a career in television, where he made a lot of money. One time he came home for a visit, and he was stopped on the street by an old boyhood friend who had turned into the town panhandler. He told the television star all of his troubles and then asked him for a loan. The television star had listened to the panhandler's sad story, but in the end told him no. The old bum looked at him and said, "Well, there's one thing they can truthfully say about you. Success hasn't changed you one bit."

In every sales meeting there is room for a word about *enthusiasm*, the greatest single word in selling. Along with your serious illustrations about the value of enthusiasm, slip in a few funny stories:

When I was growing up I used to hang around the local hardware store. I finally was given the job of sweeping out the place. I learned a lot, working for that old hardware dealer. One time he called in one of his clerks and said to him, "Wilbur, you are the best salesman I've got. You are the first one in every morning and the last one to leave at night. I have never seen you idle one minute. When you are not waiting on customers you are putting up new stock and keeping the store neat and attractive. No detail seems to escape your notice. And for those reasons I'm afraid I'm going to have to fire you." "Fire me!" the clerk shouted. "If I'm all that good, why are you going to fire me?" "Because," the boss said, "it's somebody like you, full of enthusiasm, who will eventually go out and start your own business in competition with me."

That's where I also learned about "reverse enthusiasm." One old fellow named Rufus worked there. He wasn't any good at all. He was lazy and shiftless and never did anything right. One day he quit. A few days later, a friend of his was in the store and noticed he wasn't there and said, "Where's Rufus?" And the boss told him that Rufus had quit. "Who you gonna get to fill his vacancy?" the man asked. And the boss told him, "When Rufus left, he didn't leave a vacancy."

You've got to be eager. You've got to show enthusiasm or you'll never get the job done. Three boy scouts had been sent out from the scout meeting to perform their good deed for the day. In about fifteen minutes they came back and reported that they had all done their good deed. "We helped a little old lady across the street," they said. The scoutmaster was dumbfounded and said, "You mean to tell me that all three of you helped the same little old lady across the street. It certainly didn't take all three of you to help her." "Oh, yes, it did," one of the scouts said, "because she didn't want to cross the street."

A budding young architect was telling his girl friend about a new church he had just designed. "You should see the beautiful new altar in the sanctuary," he said. And her voice was full of enthusiasm when she said, "Lead me to it."

The stories about salesmen are endless. You can always find plenty of funny ones to fit any sales message you are trying to put across.

FOR A SAFETY MEETING

Here is a laughter-filled routine that is appropriate for a safety meeting. "The minister at our church was visiting the prisoners at the county jail, and he was chatting with a man who had been sentenced for safecracking. He said to him, 'Now that you have had some time to meditate and think about the mistake you made, I hope you have decided to correct your faults.' 'I sure have,' the safe-cracker said. 'From now on when I pull a job, I'm going to wear gloves.' Don't be like that man. Don't learn the hard way. Always wear your gloves, and safety glasses and . . .'"

Emphatic points in a speech are best made with short, pithy sentences. After you have made your point, tell your audience a story as an illustration. "Always play it safe. If you are getting a shave, talk to the barber about the weather. It's dangerous to discuss anything as exciting as football or politics with a man who has a razor in his hand."

In the next example, the point is made both before and after the story.

"Every now and then you will find someone who isn't in accord with your safety program. Don't let it worry you. Don't let it stop you. Back home when I was a boy, a traveling salesman checked into our little old three-story hotel. Along with his suitcase there was a large coil of rope. 'What's the rope for?' the desk clerk asked him. 'Oh,' the salesman said, 'that's my fire escape. I always carry it with me. There have been a lot of hotel fires recently, and I don't want to take any chances. In case of fire I just let myself down from the window.' 'That's a good plan,' the desk clerk said, 'but all guests who bring their own fire escapes have to pay in advance at this hotel.' That salesman had a good safety idea, but the hotel desk clerk just wasn't in sympathy with it."

A minor point can sometimes be made with a fast quip. "One big problem in putting over your safety program is lack of communication. Tell your story so that it will be remembered. Here is one I'll remember for a long time. Driving into town this morning I came up behind a truck with this sign on the back: This truck has had six accidents and hasn't lost a one.'"

THE FUND-RAISING CAMPAIGN

Sooner or later, every public speaker will find himself involved in a fund-raising drive. Here are several stories that can be altered to suit a fund-drive speech. You might even tell them one after the other as your opening routine.

I'm going to open this drive by asking the $64,000 question. Is there anybody here who will give us $64,000? As you workers go out to raise money, you'll hear every excuse in the world, even the famous old excuse that W. C. Fields used when people tried to squeeze a donation out of him. Fields would say, "I'm sorry but I find myself in a most embarrassing situation. All of my available assets at the moment are tied up in ready cash."

Last year, when I was captain of one of the teams, I sent one of my best workers to call on a well-to-do businessman. He came back without a contribution. I sent out two more men, and they came back empty-handed too. Finally, when I was having a team meeting, I told them I'd show them how to do it. We'd all go together to see the man. That way I figured he couldn't turn us down. And that's what we did. When we got to his office, he invited us in. "Sit down," he said. "I know why you are here. You want to know why I am not giving to the Community Fund. I suppose you have a right to know, although I don't like to discuss my private troubles in public. What you don't know is that my brother is an alcoholic. He is married and has seven children. He and his family live out

West. It's a terrible case. He hasn't earned a cent in over five years. Then there's my wife's brother. He was so badly wounded in the war that he draws 100-percent disability insurance. But with eleven children, that isn't enough money even to feed them. And because of all the children, his wife can't work. Besides that misfortune, there is my mother-in-law. She is an invalid. She has been bedridden for years. She has to have a trained nurse around the clock. And you know good and well that if I'm not helping them, I am not going to give anything to the Community Fund."

We called on another wealthy old fellow last year. I knew he was stingy. I knew I was going to have a hard time with him so I thought I'd impress him with the success we were having. I said to him, "We are out to raise $250,000 and already a well-known philanthropist in town has donated a quarter of that." "Wonderful," he said. "I'll match his contribution. I'll give you another quarter. Do you have change of a dollar?"

When I was a boy, I remember the strong man who came to town with the circus. He had a fabulous act. He could bend iron bars and twist horseshoes and do all sorts of fancy stunts. Part of his act involved audience participation. He would take a lemon and squeeze it with one hand. I never saw anything like it. He would squeeze that lemon until every single drop of juice was out of it, and nothing was left but a handful of dry pulp. [Hold up a squeezed fist.] Then he would offer anyone five dollars a drop for each drop of juice he could squeeze out of the lemon. He was famous for that act. Nobody was ever able to win anything from the strong man until he hit our town. I remember the day. When he challenged the crowd, a little sixty-five-year-old man who weighed about 135 pounds came forward. Everybody laughed until that fellow took hold of the lemon and gave it a quick squeeze and got six more drops of juice out of it. The strong man paid him without any fuss, but he said to the little man, "Who in the world are you? You must be a famous strong man in disguise. Are you with a circus? Who are you, anyway?" "Oh," the man said, "I'm not a circus strong man. I'm just the chairman of the local Community Fund Drive."

FOR AN AUDIENCE OF YOUNGSTERS

It is not always easy to win an audience of school-age youngsters. Remember that youngsters today don't usually laugh at the same stories you enjoyed when you were a kid. Changes in vocabulary and differences in style of living account for this. For example, you might have a funny old story about a gentleman who got on a Pullman in Richmond and said to the conductor . . . You won't get a ripple of laughter, because probably none of the teen-agers has ever ridden on a Pullman train. They don't even know what a Pullman is, and to them a conductor is someone who leads a band. Yet you can make that story fit by saying, "The other day I got on a bus and said to the bus driver . . ."

Use a few of their latest pet words and phrases and you will build a quick and solid rapport with your audience. Make sure, though, that you keep abreast of the current slang expressions. You can improve your chances of success if you listen to the local radio disc jockey or one of the weekly television teen-age shows.

Deliver stories as though they happened to you that very day, on the way to or after arriving at their school. Here is a five-minute routine that will rally the youngsters to your side and get them into the mood for listening to the serious part of your address.

I wasn't sure what time I was supposed to speak so I came early to be sure I would be on time. While I was waiting, your principal, Mr. Williams, showed me around the building. As we were walking down the hall we were behind two pretty little girls. I overheard them talking about a couple who passed by holding hands. "Don't you think those two are made for each other?" the first girl said. "I certainly do," her friend replied. "She's a pill, and he's a headache."

Mr. Williams took me to the cafeteria and we had a cup of coffee together. I heard one young fellow say to the boy he was sitting with, "Why in the world do you hate school so much?" And his friend said, "I don't hate school. I just hate the principle of the thing."

At the next table a young man was reading a book and one of the fellows yelled at him, "What are you reading?" "A mystery book," the other fellow said. "A mystery book? What's the title?" And the boy with the book said, *Second-Year Algebra*. It's fun to do a little eavesdropping. I overheard a girl say to a boy sitting next to her, "My boyfriend kissed me a hundred times last night. Can you beat that?" "I'm not sure," he said, "but I'm willing to try."

Tell your audience about another school you visited. "Last week I was visiting an elementary school and I sat in on a couple of the classes. I watched a teacher giving an arithmetic lesson. She was trying to explain the meaning of the word 'difference' as it is used in arithmetic. She drew seven circles on the board and said to the students, 'Watch as I erase four of the circles. Now, Billy, tell me, what is the difference?' And Billy stood up and said, 'That's what I say, what's the difference? Who cares?' Then she said to another boy, 'If you had two dimes and a nickel in one pocket and three pennies and a quarter in your other pocket, what would you have?' And he said, 'I'd have on somebody else's pants.' Then I went into a classroom where the teacher was teaching English. She said to a little girl, 'Please correct this sentence: "It was me who broke the window."' And the little girl corrected it by saying, 'It wasn't me who broke the window.'"

"Before I start my speech I want to say that I think you young people of today are very responsible. I think you have great ideas. I am proud to think that before long you will be running the world and that the destiny of our great country will be in your responsible hands. Now that I have paid you that great compliment, I hope whoever is responsible will put the hub caps back on my car. As I said, before I begin my speech I have some advice for you. The first has to do with television. Remember this. The students who watch television every night will go down in history. They'll also go down in English, algebra and chemistry. Here's the second bit of advice. It has to do with the care of the teeth. There are three rules for the proper care of the teeth. First, brush after every meal. Second, see your dentist twice a year. And third, watch out for kids who push and shove at the drinking fountain."

Make your humor fit the age group of your listeners and you'll have an attentive audience. No youngster is going to shuffle his feet or whisper to his neighbor if he thinks he's going to miss hearing something funny.

FOR THE GOLF-AWARDS BANQUET

A public speaker who is also an avid golfer is the man who is called upon to serve as toastmaster at the annual golf tournament banquet. When it is your turn, do yourself proud with a well-organized routine of golf stories.

First, tell a couple on yourself, then one or two stories about some of the winners. Along the way you can sprinkle in a few good golf jokes. Here is the type of routine you might put together.

It's a great honor to have been invited to make the golf awards tonight. I was selected because I am not eligible for any of the prizes myself. The committee said it wouldn't be fair. Like this afternoon, for example, I shot a 68. Tomorrow I'm going to play the second hole. I must say I enjoyed the tournament. I actually had a gallery watching me play. A lady and her little girl. They were watching me when I was having a bad time in the rough. I stopped once to catch my breath, and I heard the little girl say to her mother, "Oh, Mommy, I think he killed it. He's quit beating it."

But now to the winners. I was on the fourth green with [name three players] and just as we were getting ready to putt, a ball plopped down from out of no-where and rolled right up to the pin. It stopped about a foot away. [Name] said, "Hey, who did that? Who-ever it was, he sure is lucky. Let's have some fun with him. Let's kick it in the hole and when he gets here he'll think he got a hole-in-one." And that's what we did. Then, in about two minutes, up came [name], all out of breath. "Anybody seen my ball?" he yelled. "Sure," we told him. "It went in the hole." You should have seen him. He jumped up and down and screamed and clapped his hands and said, "Oh, this is great. This is the happiest day of my life. I made a nine." And so, [same name], come up here and get your prize. [Then mention the other winners.]

Boy, the judges were strict. We were on the first tee and [name] was getting ready to give the ball a mighty swing when one of the judges rushed up and shouted, "Wait a minute there. You're twelve feet in front of the marker. Get back where you belong or you'll be disqualified." And [name] really told him off. He said, "Go back and sit down. This is my third stroke."

One time there was a golf-playing Bishop. He loved the game. He always carried his clubs around in the trunk of his car and he played every chance he got. Last year, he decided to give up playing golf during Lent. Everything was fine for the first week, and then one day he was driving by a golf course. It was a beautiful day, and he couldn't resist the temptation. He said to himself, "I think I'll just hit a few practice balls to keep my game in shape. It really isn't the same as playing because I'll be by myself." So he parked his car and started playing on about the fourth hole. The next thing he knew, he was going the whole route, playing by himself. He didn't know it, but he was being observed. A little angel up in heaven was watching him. Finally, the angel went to see the Lord and said, "Lord, look down there. There's the Bishop. He's breaking his vow for Lent. I think we ought to punish him. What do you think?" And the Lord said, "I think you are right. We should teach him a lesson." And the angel said, "What do you want me to do? Strike him dead with lightning, maybe?" "No," said the Lord. "I have a better idea. Watch me. I'll punish him." At that moment the Bishop was on the sixth tee. This was a 450-yard dog leg. The Bishop took a mighty swing at the ball and away it went. Up, up, and up over the trees straight for the pin. And he did it. A hole-in-one! And the little angel said to the Lord, "Look at that. A 450-yard hole-in-one. Do you call that punishment?" "Yes," said the Lord. "For a golfer, that is the worst punishment possible. The Bishop has just hit the greatest shot in the history of golf, and he can't tell anybody about it."

The other day I was watching [name of the pro] giving some lessons to one of the new schoolteachers who had recently moved to town. They were on the green and she said to him, "I want to be sure I'm correct. What we are getting ready to do now—is it spelled p-u-t or p-u-t-t?" And he told her, "It's p-u-t-t. P-u-t means to place something exactly where you want it. P-u-t-t means a frustrating attempt to do it."

I was in the pro shop and overhead two of the ladies when they came in. One of them said to [name of the pro], "I want you to meet my friend, Mrs. Harrison. She wants to learn to play golf." "That's great," the pro said. "Do you want a lesson too?" "No," the first lady said. "I learned last week."

Write your own routine, using the names of the winners—and losers. Practice it well, and you'll be the hit of the banquet.

FOR THE COMPANY-AWARDS BANQUET

Company banquets can be great fun. In some cases you may find that employees are a bit reluctant to poke fun or laugh at the boss. However, it's always acceptable to josh the recipient of an award. A funny story tempers the solemnity of the occasion and will make the banquet much more lively. Here are a few stories that you can weave into a routine.

Tonight the grand award goes to George. Everybody knows that so there isn't any reason to be dramatic and mention his name at the end of the introduction. The other employees have been talking about it for a week.

I overheard a fellow saying the other day, "What about old George winning the big award this year? He sure is lucky, isn't he?" And his friend said, "He sure is. And you know, a funny thing about old George: the harder he works, the luckier he gets."

Speaking of luck, two little girls were playing in their mother's bedroom. They were roughhousing around, and one of them threw a shoe and broke her mother's full-length mirror. There was a big crash. Almost instantly the little girls heard their mother rush out of the kitchen. The little girl who did not throw the shoe said to her sister, "Oh, look what you did. Now you're going to have bad luck for the next seven years." And the other little girl said, "I'm not worried about the next seven years. I'm worried about the next seven minutes."

Whenever I think about luck, I always think about the luckiest person in the world, my wife. [This story should be told when your wife is seated at the head table and is wearing her mink stole.] She was hoping it would be air-conditioned tonight so she could wear her mink stole. And it was. She loves that mink stole. Last year when we were at a convention in Miami Beach, the first prize at the big banquet was a mink stole. She had always wanted a mink stole, but we never thought she would get one that easily. Oh, they didn't draw her name. Oh, no. A lady from Cincinnati won the mink stole. My little wife was lucky when the dinner was over and we were leaving. I tripped and fell down the stairs and broke my ankle. And I collected eight hundred dollars from the insurance company and brought her a mink stole.

At company parties, there is no end of stories you can tell on individuals. In a situation where everyone knows one another, string together a series of stories about your friends and you'll make a big hit. The fellow who receives the thirty-five-year award makes an excellent target:

When Harry came to work here thirty-five years ago he had been out of work for six months. His next-door neighbor said to his wife, "I hear your husband has finally found a job." "That's right," Harry's wife said. "It's hard work, and Harry says it's killing him, but thank goodness it's permanent." The first day he worked here the boss told him, "To start, your job will be half indoors and half outdoors." And Harry said to the boss, "That's all right with me, but what happens if somebody slams the door?"

Harry is getting his thirty-five-year pin tonight. He doesn't even look thirty-five, does he? [Applaud, and everybody will applaud with you.] I asked him the other day how old he was and he said he was thirty-two. And I said, "That's impossible. If you're only thirty-two, how were you able to work for thirty-five years?" "Oh," he said, "I've put in a lot of overtime." Yes, Harry has been with the company for thirty-five years. It wasn't easy for him to settle down and go to work. When he applied to personnel for a job he asked them, "How much do you pay?" And they told him the usual plan: "We pay you sixty-five dollars a week now. Six months from now we will pay you seventy-five dollars a week." And Harry said, "That sounds great. I'll be back in six months and take the job."

Stories in which you can insert the names of your fellow employees are endless. All you have to do is work them together to create a smooth routine.

FOR THE SECRETARIES' CLUB

Secretaries often invite men to speak at their luncheons. Usually the guest speaker is the boss of one of the members. When you have received such an invitation, be sure to have some complimentary stories about secretaries. Here is a sample routine of funny stories that reflects credit on the girls.

When Miss Carrie asked me to speak to the secretaries' club today I asked her what her definition of a secretary was. This is what she told me: "A secretary is a woman who is supposed to look like a movie star, typewrite like a machine, remember like a computer, act like a lady, think like a man and work like a dog." I told my secretary, Ellen, about this. Last year we heard a rumor that Ellen was planning to quit. And the men in the office gave notice that they were going on strike. When I asked why, they said, "Because Ellen is leaving. We've always considered her charm, beauty and personality as some of our fringe benefits."

A man couldn't get along in business without a wise secretary. A few weeks ago, Ellen came in and said, "There's a man out front to see you. He says he's here to collect some money you owe him." And I said, "What does he look like?" And Ellen said, "He looks like you'd better pay him." I remember the first day Ellen came to work for me. I asked her if she was tactful and if she understood the fundamentals of public relations. She said she knew what I was talking about. That very afternoon, she had a chance to show me her skills. An attractive lady came in and asked if I was in. "Oh, yes," she said. "He's in and I'm sure he'll see you right away. He never keeps a beautiful woman waiting." Of course, that lady happened to be my wife.

Over the years, Ellen has developed a keen understanding of public relations and what to tell people. Now when people call or come by, this is the system she uses. If it's nine o'clock and I've not arrived at the office, she says, "He's not in his office at the moment, but I expect him back in a few minutes." If I've still not come by ten o'clock, she says, "He's gone out, but I expect him to return shortly." If I'm still not at work by eleven o'clock, she says, "He went to lunch early. May I take a message?" If I still haven't come to work by two o'clock, she says, "He's not back from lunch yet. May I take a message?" And if I haven't come in by three o'clock, she says, "He's gone for the day." When I've taken off to play golf, she tells people, "He's out with three clients traversing eighteen segments of important real estate." And when I've sneaked off to go fishing, she says, "He's out of the office for the rest of the day working on a marine biology project."

You will notice that in the routine about secretaries, you do not make fun of the girls as you did of your fellow employees at the company party. If you flatter the girls, your speech will be a huge success and you will be invited back.

This is a summary of the rules for telling funny stories successfully.

The DO's will help to improve your platform performance. Study these rules. Apply them. Practice them. And you will develop into a skillful public speaker.

When you tell your funny story:

Do learn it. Be sure you know the story backward and forward, inside and out. Have the punch line so well memorized that you can't possibly forget or fumble it.

Do make it sound like the truth. Remember that sincerity is the single most important element in public speaking. Your story must sound sincere or it will have a hollow ring.

Put your own personality into the story. Remember that people came to hear you speak; to hear you tell them the truth; not to hear you relate several stories you read in a joke book in a library. If the audience believes that the story really happened, they will listen more attentively and half of your battle will be won.

Do keep it short. Keep to the point. Use only the words that are necessary to the story and forget the extraneous matter. Include only the information that bears directly on the punch line.

Do keep it clean. One touch of offensive humor can destroy an entire speech.

Do dramatize it. Act out your story. Gesticulate and shout or whisper. Use appropriate facial expressions. Remember that you are putting on a show, so put on a good one.

Do tell it. Heed the rule against reading a funny story.

Do enjoy it. Let your audience know you are happy to be there and that you are enjoying yourself. Be gay. Be vivacious. Spread good cheer.

Do speak distinctly. Make sure that everyone in the room can hear every word you say. It's difficult enough to make an audience laugh when they hear and understand you, but it's impossible if you aren't audible. Too often when people are laughing at a story, someone will lean over and say to a neighbor, "I didn't get it, what did he say?" Be sure none of your listeners has that trouble.

Do deliver the punch line deliberately. It is much more effective if you slow down, though not noticeably so, and raise your voice slightly when you deliver your punch line. Sometimes you can get by if you tell a story like an amateur, but you must always deliver the punch line like an old pro.

Do speak with poise. Stand in a comfortable position. Use your hands to illustrate your story instead of putting them awkwardly in your pockets or using them to hang onto the lectern as though you were riding a bicycle.

Do practice. The most important step toward perfection in public speaking is practice. You can't practice too much. After you have the story exactly the way you want it, practice it. Practice. Practice. Practice.

And just to keep you alert to the pitfalls in public speaking, here are a few DONT's.

These are the mistakes to avoid. They mark the inept speaker and distinguish the amateur from the professional. If you are planning to tell funny stories, take these negative rules seriously. Any one of these mistakes can harm your speech; some of them can be fatal.

When you tell your funny story:

Don't read it. If you have to read your story, you have failed to follow the basic rule of being funny—you don't know your story. Never use a story in your speech that you don't know well enough to tell from memory.

This error seems so obvious that you may wonder why it is even mentioned. However, it must not be quite so evident since speakers make this mistake every day. Not long ago I saw a banquet chairman attempt to close a meeting with a big laugh after a speech by one of America's most popular humorists. This was a mistake in itself, but to make things worse, the chairman said, "Before we adjourn, I have a couple of jokes here." He proceeded to read two rather dull stories. Nobody laughed. He was embarrassed and said, "Well, they must not be so funny, so I'll skip the other two I have written down." Still nobody laughed. He did manage to save the day by being himself and acting natural. He stood there for a moment looking sick. He was not pretending either. Then he said, "My wife, Ruth, told me not to read those jokes. She said if I did, I'd make a fool of myself." Then he looked down at her, sitting at the head table, and said, "So I did, and I did." He was telling the truth. And the truth was funny. And everybody laughed.

Moreover, there is a big difference between spoken English and written English. All speeches should be given in spoken English. When you read a funny story, you are trying to hurdle some formidable obstacles. The jokes and funny stories that you find in humor books are in written English. They have to be translated into your own everyday vocabulary before you can deliver them properly. However, the biggest drawback when you read anything, especially a funny story, is that you will sound stiff and dull, and bore the audience.

Don't announce it. You will destroy the priceless element of surprise if you announce to your audience that you are about to tell a funny story. Don't say, "That reminds me of a funny story." Go ahead and tell it. If you tell it properly and it fits the point, your audience will see the connection. You won't have to clarify it for them.

Then, too, if you have announced that you are going to be funny and are not quite as funny as you predicted, you will have experienced a setback.

Therefore, when it comes time to tell your funny story, tell it. If it turns out to be "not so funny," you really do not lose much because you did not promise anybody anything to laugh at. In this situation, the best rule is to ignore your attempt at being funny—just as the audience ignored it.

There are times, however, when you have obviously tried to raise a laugh and your story falls so flat that it can't be ignored. If this should happen to you, don't scold the audience for not laughing. Rather, take the blame yourself. Here is one way to do it. "I should have known better than to tell that story. I told it about six weeks ago when I spoke in Harlan, Kentucky. Nobody laughed then, either. But I figured they didn't laugh because I was in a remote part of the mountains of Kentucky. I didn't like them not laughing, so I said, 'Well, you folks will probably laugh at that one about six weeks after I have gone.' And right away a voice from the back of the room said, 'No, sir. We laughed at it six weeks before you got here.'"

Don't fumble it. A funny story should be an integral part of your speech and not a separate item that seems to be tacked onto it. When it is time to deliver the story, tell it without any preliminary hemming and hawing. Move into it smoothly, with no giveaway signals. Do it the same way that a star quarterback makes a sneak hand-off. His action is so slick that it appears effortless. His aim is to hand off that ball so skillfully that his movement is unnoticeable. Just let him fumble the ball a bit and he's in trouble. The same is true with storytelling. Sometimes it takes only one fumble to cost you the game.

Don't explain it. If you tell a story and nobody laughs, don't try to salvage the story with an explanation. That only makes things worse. When you explain a story, you are admitting that either you weren't adept enough to tell it properly or that you think your listeners were too dull to understand it. Either approach tends to diminish your stature in the audience's eyes. Maybe they did "get it," but they didn't think much of it.

Don't apologize for it. Don't kill all the laugh potentials by downgrading your story. Don't say, "Maybe you have heard the story I'm going to tell, and maybe it really isn't very funny," or "I might not tell it very well, but anyway, they told me that I ought to have some funny stories in my speech, so here it is." Or "I thought I'd end my speech with a funny story. Even though it's pretty old, I'm going to tell it anyway."

If you think these are absurd examples, just start listening carefully to speakers who are trying to be funny and you'll see how often these apologies are used.

Don't move too fast. Many funny stories are ruined

because the storyteller hasn't sufficiently prepared the audience for the punch line. In other words, there is no build-up. For example, if you wanted your wife to get the most excitement out of receiving a gift of perfume, you wouldn't pull an unwrapped package from your pocket and unceremoniously thrust it at her. Instead, you would have the package gift-wrapped so that she could anticipate the surprise while she was unwrapping it. Then her eyes would light up and her hands would tremble and she would be emotionally prepared for the final unveiling of her gift.

For the same reason, stories should be placed in a setting and background. The audience should be prepared for the punch line.

Don't risk the risqué. Many a speaker has ruined an otherwise prize-winning speech by peppering it with offensive humor. Determining what might or might not be offensive is a matter of judgment. Yet sometimes it is difficult to judge your own speech. Even if nobody laughed at your story, you might not know the reason for the silence. You might say to yourself, "That audience was pretty dull. They missed that story completely." Or if your story brought down the house, you might conclude, "Boy, I was a little afraid of that one, but I got by with it after all."

You may be wrong in both cases. Sometimes people keep quiet because they disapprove of a story. And even if half of the audience laughed heartily, you still might be offending the other half. If you offend only one or two persons in your audience, you have made a blunder.

What, then, is a good rule to follow?

Never tell a story that can offend.

This eliminates all risqué stories. Keep away from sex. Even the "cute" story that was whispered to you in private an hour before the banquet by the chairman himself might offend him if you told it for all to hear.

This raises the question of personal humor. It is quite acceptable as long as the person you are kidding is present and he is well known and liked. Using personal humor requires careful selection of the stories and great skill in handling them. The humor should be exaggerated rather than direct and cutting. A good example would be to josh the newly elected president of a group about railroading the election if he had been nominated without opposition and elected by acclamation. However, you would be on extremely dangerous ground telling the same story if someone had just lost the election to him by a margin of two or three votes.

In a well-balanced twenty-minute speech there is room for only about five stories at the most. With the thousands of side splitters to choose from, why not tell a couple of jokes on yourself and then you will have only three more stories to work on. If you cannot find three inoffensive funny stories, then you had better keep away from humor entirely.

Don't gamble. Don't tell a story that you don't think is funny. If you didn't laugh when you first heard it, the chances are that nobody will laugh when you tell it. Even if it is a funny story, you won't be able to deliver it well if you don't have a special "feeling" for it.

Don't laugh at your own story. Laughing at something you have said is the mark of a rank amateur. It is no more proper to laugh at your own humor than it would be to applaud yourself. Let your audience decide whether or not you have done a good job. You do the telling and let them do the laughing.

Don't fail to practice. No matter how many rules you learn about humor, the only way to become proficient in the art of telling stories is to practice.